The London BABY Directory™ 2001-2002

An A-Z of EVERYTHING
for
pregnant women, babies and children

edited by
Karen Liebreich

First published 1997
Second edition updated 1998
Third edition updated 1999
Fourth edition updated 2000
Fifth edition updated 2001

by The Baby Directory Limited
10 Grove Park Terrace, London W4 3QG. 020 8742 8724

ISBN 1-903288-00-2

© Karen Liebreich

Designed by LB Graphics, 01795 428150
Printed and bound in Great Britain by AOK Printers & Stationers, 01689 891460

covers
all Central and Greater London

Local Baby Directories now available:

Bristol & Bath

Herts & Middlesex

Oxfordshire, Berks & Bucks

South Wales

Surrey & S.Middlesex

Sussex & Hampshire

Franchise possibilities

If there is no Baby Directory in your area and you think
there should be,
contact us to discuss franchise opportunities.

Visit our website for

■ The Baby Directory Encyclopaedia of Pregnancy & Birth ■
■ Medical Advice ■ Breastfeeding ■
■ Educational Advice ■
■ The Baby Directory Shop - all your nursery needs ■
■ Book Shop ■ Prizes ■ Updates ■

Karen Liebreich is editor of The London Baby Directory and
www.babydirectory.com, as well as supervising editor of The Local
Baby Directories. She is the author of a book of history stories for
children, UneXplained (Macmillan). She is also the author of *Doing
Business in Eastern Europe* and *The Complete Skier* (BBC Books), which is
now www.ifyouski.com, the leading European ski web site. She was
chair of the Central London branch of the National Childbirth Trust
and served several years on various maternity hospital and health
authority committees. She has two children.

Acknowledgements

The Baby Directory would like to thank the following people for their help:

Web master: *Paul Kriwaczek*
Designer: *Sioux Peto*
Assistant editor: *Kitty Liebreich*
Regional editor: *Charlotte Barney*
Mail order editor: *Sarah Coyle*
Researcher: *Margaret Oszust*
Computer consultant: *Jeremy Levy*
Book deliveries: *Zero Emissions*
Accountancy services: *Dominique Simpson*
Legal advice: *Bird & Bird, Debbie Ruff*
Initial inspiration: *Sam and Hannah*

And to all those who have sent in suggestions, or checked sections, *many thanks!*

Welcome to the fifth edition of The London Baby Directory. The original Directory, published in 1997, arose after years of collecting information on scraps of paper torn out of magazines, or scribbled on the back of old envelopes, never to be found to hand when the need arose, so we finally got our act together and compiled all the information into a book. Now we cover most of SE England, Bristol and South Wales and are spreading fast.

The aim of the Baby Directories is to provide you with one convenient source of information for all your needs while pregnant, or as a parent or carer with a baby or child.

We have made no quality judgements about the entrants, except that where we have heard bad rumours - confirmed by several readers - about a product or service, we have not included it. This is pretty rare, and does not imply that we have tested or approved all the remaining entrants. The advertisers paid to be included, the listings were all free.

If you find errors or omissions, please let us know. Many thanks to those of you who responded with information - your free copies are on their way to you.

Our web site at **www.babydirectory.com** now includes our own **Encyclopaedia of Pregnancy and Birth**, as well as updated listings for the whole country, free medical advice, an excellent book shop and our *new* **Baby Directory Shop**, one of the best places to buy all your baby stuff.

We hope you find The London Baby Directory useful.

Karen Liebreich
Editor
editor@babydirectory.com

note to advertisers

The Baby Directories are compiled
during autumn each year and
published in spring
**Deadline for acceptance is
10th January**

Contact us for further details:
020 8742 8724
e-mail: editor@babydirectory.com
or see feedback page

Best feedback:

Many thanks to:
Karen Dobres, Elena Edwards, Fi Gillingham
and Fabienne Naconzi for sending in great
feedback. Free copies for them - remember to
send in yours.

Order form 2001-2002

To order, call our Credit Card hotline on **020 8742 8724**
or fax us on **020 8580 7085** *or* order via our secure website at **www.babydirectory.com**
or send this order form with your payment to:
The London Baby Directory, 10 Grove Park Terrace, London W4 3QG

Title	Price	Qty	Postage	Total
The London Baby Directory (1-903288-00-2)	**£6.99**		**£1.50**	
The Local Baby Directory				
Bristol & Bath (1-903288-04-5)	£4.99		£1.00	
Herts & Middlesex (1-903288-01-0)	£4.99		£1.00	
Oxfordshire, Berks & Bucks (1-903288-02-9)	£4.99		£1.00	
South Wales (1-903288-06-1)	£4.99		£1.00	
Surrey & S. Middlesex (1-903288-03-7)	£4.99		£1.00	
Sussex & Hampshire (1-903288-05-3)	£4.99		£1.00	
		Total Order Value		

Please print clearly
Name . . . .

Address . . . .

. . . .

. . . . Postcode . . . .

Tel . . . . E-mail address . . . .

METHOD OF PAYMENT *(please tick appropriate box)*
Cheque/Postal Order ☐   Credit Card ☐

Please make cheques payable to **The London Baby Directory**

Card Number ☐☐☐☐ ☐☐☐☐ ☐☐☐☐ ☐☐☐☐ ☐☐☐☐

Issue No ☐☐   Expiry Date ☐☐☐☐   Valid from ☐☐☐☐

Signature . . . .

Code . . . .   If you do not wish to receive further information please tick ☐

ADVERTISERS

If you provide a service or product we should know about, drop us a line, fax or e-mail. Listings are free, but we offer great advertising deals!

☐ This is a new product, service or facility.

☐ Please contact me with more information about advertising.

☐ I wish to re-book (before August 2001) at 2000-2001 prices!!

☐ Oops! You've missed this.

☐ Change of address, new branch, etc.

Category of product (eg, park, restaurant, nursery) ....

Name of product, service or facility ....

Address ....

....

Postcode .... Tel No ....

E-mail address .... www ....

Contact name and tel no *(if different from above)*

....

READERS

We would very much appreciate your comments. Errors, omissions, or poor service, please let us know. **A free copy of next year's book for the most useful comments!**

Feedback ....

....

....

....

Your own name, address, 'phone number, e-mail address (all optional)

....

....

Many thanks for taking the time to fill in this form

Please send completed form(s) to:

The London Baby Directory, 10 Grove Park Terrace, London W4 3QG

Tel: 020 8742 8724   Fax: 020 8580 7085   E-mail: editor@babydirectory.com

ACUPUNCTURE
By Sam Levy

acupuncture

(see also complementary health)

Some recommend acupuncture in pregnancy for morning sickness and turning breech babies.

British Acupuncture Council
63 Jeddo Road, London W12. 020 8735 0400
Ring for list of practitioners

Zita West
020 7467 8475
www.zitawest.com

adventure playgrounds

(see also indoor adventure playcentres, parks & playgrounds)

These are usually for 5 years and above. For the junior version, see one o'clock clubs.

E2
Apples & Pears Playground
28 Pearson Street. 020 7729 6062

E10
Brooks Farm
Skeltons Lane Park, Leyton. 020 8539 4278

N19
Timbuktu Playground
Grenville Road. 020 7272 2183
5-14yrs

SE23
Home Park Adventure Playground
Winchfield Road. 020 8659 2329
Closed Monday

SW9
Loughborough Centre
Moorland Road. 020 7926 1049

a

SW11
Battersea Park Adventure Playground
Sun Gate Entrance (Prince of Wales Drive),
Albert Bridge Road. 020 8871 7539

York Gardens Adventure Playground
York Gardens, Lavender Road.
020 7223 3269

SW18
Kimber BMX/Adventure Playground
Kimber Road. 020 8870 2168
5-16yrs

W5
Log Cabin Adventure Playground
259 Northfield Avenue. 020 8840 1806

W6
Kids and Co Adventure Playground
Distillery Lane. 020 8748 9224
5yrs+

W12
White City Adventure Playground
Canada Way, White City Estate.
020 8749 0909
5-12yrs

TW9
Marble Hill Adventure Playground
Marble Hill Park, Richmond Road,
Twickenham.
April - Sept. Small charge. 5-15yrs

Richmond Adventure Playground
behind Pools in the Park, Old Deer Park,
Twickenham Road

WWW. BABY directory.com
Come and visit us

a after school clubs

Many schools run after school clubs for their own and external pupils, usually from 3.30-6pm. Try your child's school, your local school, or ring the local Youth Service (*see councils*).

Kids' Club Network Helpline
020 7512 2100

Kumon Educational
0800 854 714
www.kumon.co.uk
See advert on page 92

NW1
Camden Play Service
218 Everold Street. 020 7974 1519

NW10
Brent
Units 23-28 Bridge Park, Brentfield, Harrow Road. 020 8881 9126

SE1/SE15/SE19
Club Lighthouse
020 8761 6006
4-12yrs

SE23
Pavilion Kids' Club
c/o Cottage Day Nursery. 020 8291 7117
4-11yrs

SW19
Dundonald After School Club
Dundonald First School, Dundonald Road.
020 8542 5685
4-10yrs

W5
Ealing Play Services
020 8280 1030

aikido

Aikido for all Ages
Merton Adult College,
Whatley Avenue, SW20. 020 8543 9292
info@merton-adult-college.ac.uk
5yrs+

alexander technique

(*see also exercise classes, personal trainers*)

Society of Teachers of the Alexander Technique
020 7284 3338

antenatal support & information

(*see also hospitals, independent midwives*)

Information is available from your GP, your health clinic, the local maternity unit and the organisations listed below (some of which are commercial).

Active Birth Centre
25 Bickerton Road, London N19.
020 7482 5554

Birth Education Network
020 8995 8940
www.birthed.net

Independent Midwives' Association
1 The Great Quarry, Guildford, Surrey.
01483 821104
www.independentmidwives.org.uk

National Childbirth Trust (NCT)
Alexandra House, Oldham Terrace,
London W3. 0870 444 8707
www.nctpregnancyandbabycare.com
'Informed, unbiased information'

The Parent Company
6 Jacob's Well Mews, W1. 020 7935 0123
www.theparentcompany.co.uk
See advert under parentcraft

Portland Hospital
205-209 Great Portland Street, W1.
020 7580 4400
www.theportlandhospital.com

www.zitawest.com
See advert on page 154

Beth Pollock's Emergency Food Rescue Packs
020 7630 0695
Home-made food delivered for your first weeks at home after the birth.
See advert under food

---

antenatal teachers

(see also antenatal support & information)

Antenatal teachers are often affiliated to the National Childbirth Trust or the Active Birth Centre. Maternity hospitals usually offer classes. Book early.

Birth Preparation Programme
020 8530 1146

Fountain Clinic
020 7704 0244

E4
Arlene Dunkley Wood
020 8923 6452

E5/E9/N16
Jessica James
020 8806 4820

E17
Rose Ryan
020 8503 6807

E18/NW8
Jeyarani Gentle Birth Programme
020 8530 1146
www.jeyarani.com

KT3
Ruth Armes
020 8395 9435

North
Lynne Murphy
020 7281 7059

N1
Trish Ferguson
020 7354 5228

N14
Jill Benjoya Miller
020 8361 1433

N19
Janet Balaskas
c/o Active Birth Centre. 020 7482 5554
www.activebirthcentre.com

NW3/NW5/NW7
Yvonne Moore Birth Preparation
020 7794 2056

NW6/NW10/SW11
Julie Krausz
020 8459 2903

SW1/SW11
Lesley-Anne Kerr
Childbirth Preparation & Birth
020 7564 3316
lakerr@ultramail.co.uk

SW3
Heather Guerrini
020 7352 0245

SW4/SW11
Pitter-Patter Ante-natal Classes
020 7622 1743

SW15
Val Orrow
020 8789 8885

SW19
Mama-Rhythms
020 8879 7081

antenatal teachers (cont.)

W1/W11
Lizzie Hibbitt
020 8994 1076

W4
Christine Hill Associates
020 8994 4349

W4/W6/W12
Kerry James
020 8740 9219
www.antenatalclasses.co.uk

W11
Lolly Stirk
020 8964 1882

antenatal testing

Ask your GP or maternity unit for information. Most tests are available on the NHS.

Foetal Medical Centre
8 Devonshire Place, W1. 020 7486 0476

arabic

Arabic School in Wimbledon
Wimbledon College, Edge Hill, SW19.
01372 460 005
4-16yrs. Sats

aromatherapy

(see also complementary health, massage)

International Federation of Aromatherapists
182 Chiswick High Road, London W4.
020 8742 2605

mail order:

Aromababy
0061 39387 1999
www.aromababy.com

Aromakids
01278 671461
www.hippychickltd.co.uk

Beaming Baby
0800 0345 672
www.beamingbaby.com
Natural & Organic Products for Mother & Baby
See advert under nappies

Chawtons
01858 410886
www.chawtons.com

earth friendly baby
020 8206 2066

Earth Mother
020 8442 1704
www.earthmother-aroma.co.uk
Mail order or by 'phone

Jurlique
020 8841 6644

Natural Health Remedies
0800 074 7744
www.nhr.kz

Vital Touch
01803 840670
www.vitaltouch.com

♥ baby **WORKSHOP**® A R O M A B A B Y® ♥

The original, the purest and still the most beautiful natural skincare, accessories and gifts for Mother and Child on Earth.

All Aromababy products are 100% free from added colours, artificial perfumes, petro-chemicals, parabens, sulphates, peanut oil, talc and animal ingredients. Aromababy uses advanced mild and gentle formulations based on botanical ingredients, ensuring the absolute best for Baby's skin. Aromababy products have been used in select hospitals with much success. Products include for pregnancy, labour, prem, dad-to-be, toddler and sensitive skin. Contact our Customer Service Department for your nearest stockist. Hospital and wholesale enquiries welcome.   www.aromababy.com

Baby Gift Registry and Mail Order available +61 3 9387 1999
2B Staley Street, Brunswick Vic 3056 Australia. Email: aromababy@bigpond.com

retail:

NW3 - Verde
15 Flask Walk. 020 7431 3314

SW11 - Verde
75 Northcote Road. 020 7924 4379

other:

AromAware
The Portland Hospital for Women and Children. 020 7390 8061

www.babydirectory.com

AromAware™
CARE IN PREGNANCY

AROMATHERAPY AND YOGA IN PREGNANCY
at The Portland Hospital for Women and Children

CARE IN PREGNANCY includes
Yoga: an ideal form of exercise in pregnancy
Aromatherapy massage: combining relaxation and the therapeutic effects of essential oils
Aromaclasses: the opportunity to learn the safe and effective use of essential oils for pregnancy, labour, post-natal recovery and child-care

BABY MASSAGE COURSE
Suitable for babies from newborn to crawling.

For further information and a brochure call
020 7390 8061
CARE IN PREGNANCY is open to all women even those not receiving their obstetric care at The Portland Hospital

art

(see also dance, drama, music)

N8
Arties
020 8343 8722

N10
Colour Me Mine
452 Muswell Hill Broadway. 020 8444 6886
www.colourmemine.com

Art 4 Fun
212 Fortis Green Road. 020 8444 4333
www.Art4Fun.com

N19
Highgate Newtown
Community Centre
25 Bertram Street. 020 7272 7201
hncc@camvolsec12.demon.co.uk

NW1/W8
Nellie's young@art Classes
020 7428 7600

NW3
London International Gallery of
Children's Art
02 Centre, 255 Finchley Road. 020 7435 0903
www.ligca.org
Gallery exhibiting children's art.
Workshops

NW3/W1
Creative Wiz Kids
020 7794 6797
Parties and holiday activities too

NW6
Art 4 Fun
172 West End Lane. 020 7794 0800
www.Art4Fun.com

SE15
Ink Tank
020 7639 5611
3-11yrs. *See advert under party entertainers*

SE23
Crawley Studios
39 Wood Vale, Forest Hill. 020 8516 0002
www.crawleystudios.fsnet.co.uk

SW1
Happy Hands
55 Sloane Square, Cliveden Place.
020 7730 5544
www.happyhands.ws
Hand and foot prints and works of art
preserved on ceramic tiles

Knightsbridge Kindergarten
St. Peter's Church, Eaton Square.
020 7371 2306

SW1/SW6/SW7
Colourcraft Junior Art School
106 Warwick Way. 020 7630 0958

SW2
Tulse Hill Pottery
93 Palace Road. 020 8674 2400

SW6
JYPS
402 Lillie Road. 020 7610 2819
www.jypstshirts.com
T-shirts etc from your drawings

Splats and Splodges
Ashburnham, Tetcott Road. 020 7731 1314
4-7yrs

Mira Stevanoska's Art Classes
53 Walham Grove. 020 7386 8015
mira@portrait.co.uk

Bravura
612 Fulham Road. 020 7731 7633

Bridgewater Pottery Café
735 Fulham Road. 020 7736 2157

SW14
Art Yard
318 Upper Richmond Road West.
020 8878 1336

Studioflex
26-28 Priests Bridge. 020 8878 7753

Ceramic Magic
40 Sheen Lane. 020 8255 2484

SW18
Glazed and Amused
424 Garratt Lane. 020 8944 8060

SW19
Crafty Kids
020 8788 2637
3-10yrs

SW20
Art for Tots
01372 386 520
2-3yrs

W4
Weekly Art Clas
020 7229 1847
6-12yrs

Art and Craft Cr
Studio 6 & 7,
Turnham Green Terrace Mews.
020 7603 0410
7yrs+

Art 4 Fun
444 Chiswick High Road. 020 8994 4100
www.Art4Fun.com

W6
The Ceramics Café
215 King Street. 020 8741 4140

W8
Kids on the Hill
Etheline Holder Hall, 5b Denbigh Road.
020 8961 7014

W9
Colour Me Mine
168-170 Randolph Avenue. 020 7328 5577
www.colourmemine.com

W11
Art 4 Fun
196 Kensington Park Road

W13
Picasso's Place
6 Argyle Road. 020 8810 4422

arts centres

May also run arts, dance, drama, music classes (see these categories and also theatres).

N6
Jacksons Lane Community Centre
269a Archway Road. 020 8340 5226

NW3
Camden Arts Centre
Arkwright Road. 020 7435 2643

NW6
Tricycle Theatre
269 Kilburn High Road. 020 7328 1000

SW11
Battersea Arts Centre
Old Town Hall, Lavender Hill.
020 7223 2223

Watermans Art Centre
40 High Street, Brentford. 020 8568 1176

a   au pair agencies

(see also babysitters, childminders, mother's help, nanny agencies)

Au pairs live-in and help with housework, childcare and babysitting. They are not generally recommended for very small babies.

Au Pair International
118 Cromwell Road, SW7. 020 7370 3798

Au Pairs Worldwide
1 Aldbourne Road, W12. 020 8354 4477
aupairswor@aol.com

Friends
PO Box 22955, N10 3ZQ. 020 8444 0685

Just Help
Ken Hill House, Cricket St Thomas, nr Chard, Somerset. 01460 30775

Mar's Au Pair Agency
020 8995 6594

Montrose Agency International
23 Bullescroft Road, HA8. 020 8958 9209

b

♥ baby WORKSHOP® AUSTRALIA ♥

The original, the purest and still the most beautiful natural skincare, accessories and gifts for Mother and Child on Earth.

baby WORKSHOP offer a selection of botanical-based all-Australian skincare for mother and child, lush Australian towelling bath accessories and spa gowns, and divine 100% cotton PLAYWEAR™ mix and match garments, all available in both pure white or ivory. All-leather pull-on baby shoes in silver, gold, cream, white, snake, powder pink, pastel blue, black and brown, complete the look. Gorgeous baby-friendly bears are also available in an assortment of checks, velours, brights and natural fabrics. Contact our Customer Service Department for your nearest stockist. Wholesale enquiries welcome. www.babyworkshop.co.uk www.aromababy.com

Baby Gift Registry and Mail Order available +61 3 9387 1999
2B Staley Street, Brunswick Vic 3056 Australia. Email: aromababy@bigpond.com

baby beauty treatments

Do babies need beautifying?

Aromababy
0061 39387 1999
www.babyworkshop.com

Beaming Baby
0800 0345 672
Natural & Organic Products for Mother & Baby. *See advert under nappies*

Mini Kin
79 Fortis Green Road, N10. 020 8444 1717
Beauty salon for 0-12yrs, pregnant women

baby research

Babylab
Centre for Brain & Cognitive Development,
32 Torrington Square, WC1. 020 7631 6258

b _**C**hildminders_

London's Leading Babysitting Service · Established 1967

Locally based nurses, teachers, nannies, etc. throughout London. All sitters interviewed and referenced.

020 7935 3000

6 Nottingham Street
London W1U 5EJ

LICENSED AGENCY - ESTABLISHED 1967 - REC MEMBER

babysitters

(see also childminders, nanny agencies)

Babysitters Childminders
6 Nottingham Street, W1.
020 7935 3000
www.babysitter.co.uk

Sitters
0800 389 0038
www.sitters.co.uk

Babysitting Circle Agency
Rusthall, 230 Beechcroft Road, SW17.
020 8378 6986

Cinder's Baby Sitting Agency
020 8930 8966
www.cinder-sitters.co.uk

Please say you saw the ad in
The London Baby Directory

SitterS
0800 38 900 38
The Babysitting Service
For evening Babysitters with
Professional Childcare Experience
For more information phone us free on

REC **0800 38 900 38**
Recruitment &
Employment
Confederation
Or e-mail enquiries@sitters.co.uk.
Please quote ref: BBD
INVESTOR IN PEOPLE

Special People
Palace for All, Schofield Road, N19.
020 7686 0253
special.people@virgin.net
Specialising in special needs.
See advert under special needs

Top Notch Nannies
49 Harrington Gardens, SW7.
020 7259 2626
See advert under nanny agencies

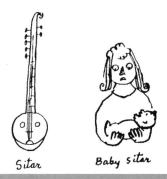

Sitar   *Baby sitar*

benefits

Benefits Agency
0541 555501
www.dss.gov.uk/ba

Maternity Alliance
45 Beech Street, Barbican, London EC2.
020 7588 8582
Advice on benefits, maternity rights at
work

birth announcements

(see also cards)

Chatterbox Cards
PO Box 142, Beckenham, Kent BR3 6ZL.
020 8650 8650
www.chatterboxcards.com

Happy Hands
55 Sloane Square, Cliveden Place,
SW1W 8AX. 020 7730 5544
www.happyhands.ws
See advert under cards

Heritage Personalised Stationery
01256 861738
www.heritage-stationery.com

boats

River Trip Information
0839 123432

b book clubs for children

Letterbox Library
71-73 Allan Road, London N16.
020 7503 4801

Red House Books Ltd
The Red House, Windrush Park,Witney,
Oxfordshire. 01993 893472

book shops for children

Major chains such as Books etc, Hammicks,
W. H. Smith, Waterstone's have good
children's sections. Visit our website at
www.babydirectory.com for a selection
of the best children's books.

E17
Hammicks
259 High Street. 020 8521 3669

N1
Angel Bookshop
102 Islington High Street. 020 7226 2904

The Bookshop Islington Green
76 Upper Street, Islington. 020 7359 4699

N10
Children's Bookshop
29 Fortis Green Road. 020 8444 5500

Muswell Hill Bookshop
72 Fortis Green Road. 020 8444 7588

N16
Stoke Newington Bookshop
159 Stoke Newington High Street.
020 7249 2808

NW1
Primrose Hill Bookshop
134 Regents Park Road. 020 7586 2022

NW3
Daunt Books
193 Haverstock Hill. 020 7794 4006

Karnac Books
118 Finchley Road. 020 7431 1075

NW5
Owl Bookshop
211 Kentish Town Road. 020 7485 7793

NW6
Kilburn Bookshop
8 Kilburn Bridge, Kilburn High Road.
020 7328 7071

West End Lane Books
277 West End Lane, West Hampstead.
020 7431 3770

NW10
Willesden Bookshop
Willesden Green Library Centre,
95 The High Road. 020 8451 7000

NW11
Bookworm
1177 Finchley Road. 020 8201 9811

SE21
The Bookshop Dulwich Village
1d Calton Avenue. 020 8693 2808

Dulwich Books Ltd
6 Croxted Road, West Dulwich.
020 8670 1920

SW1
**Harrod's Children's Book
Department**
4th floor, Harrods, Knightsbridge.
020 7225 5721

SW3
Daisy & Tom
181 King's Road. 020 7352 5000

SW6
Books for Children
97 Wandsworth Bridge Road. 020 7384 1821

Nomad Books
781 Fulham Road. 020 7736 4000

SW11
Ottakar's
6-63 St Johns Road. 020 7978 5844

Bolingbroke Bookshop
147 Northcote Road. 020 7223 9344

SW12
My Back Pages
8-10 Balham Station Road. 020 8675 9346

SW15
Ottakar's
6/6A Putney Exchange Centre.
020 8780 2401
www.ottakars.co.uk

SW17
Beckett's Bookshop
6 Bellevue Road. 020 8672 4413

SW18
Golden Treasury
27 Replingham Road, Southfields.
020 8333 0167

TW9
Kew Bookshop
1-2 Station Approach, Kew, Richmond.
020 8940 0030

W4
Bookcase
268 Chiswick High Road, W4.

W5
Children's Book Company
11 The Green. 020 8567 4324
www.childrensbookcompany.com

W8
Children's Book Centre
237 Kensington High Street. 020 7937 7497
www.childrensbookcentre.co.uk

W13
Early Bird Books
Daniel Department Store,
96 Uxbridge Road. 020 8579 0076
earlybird@bgbooksltd.fsnet.co.uk

WC2
Dorling Kindersley
10-13 King Street. 020 7836 5411

free advice from our doctor

breastfeeding accessories

(see also maternity wear)

Bravado Washable Breast Pads
020 8459 2910
www.maternitybras.co.uk

Mama Mya
0800 169 7718

Mothernature
0161 485 7359

breastfeeding advice

Visit our website at
www.babydirectory.com
for e-mail advice and information from
National Childbirth Trust and
Breastfeeding Network counsellors.

Association of Breastfeeding Mothers
020 7813 1481
abm@clara.net
24-hr volunteer counselling service

La Leche League
020 7242 1278
24-hr counselling service

NCT Breastfeeding Line
0870 4448708

SW/W
Maud Giles Lactation & Newborn Consultant
07939 820 651
maudgiles@hotmail.com

cakes

(see also party catering)

Canapes Gastronomiques
020 7794 2017
See advert under party catering

Cake Dreams
020 8889 2376

Extraordinary Cakes
020 8674 3570

KPC (Kensington Provision Company)
020 7386 7778

SW3
Jane Asher Party Cakes
22-24 Cale Street. 020 7584 6177

SW11
La Cuisiniere
81- 83, 87E/F Northcote Road.
020 7223 4487
www.la-cuisiniere.co.uk
Hire cake tins, birthday cakes, etc.
Children's cutlery

NW8
Richoux
3 Circus Road, St John's Wood.
020 7483 4001
Go for tea and order a cake

NW10
Sweet Sensation
39 Goodhall Street. 020 8838 1047

W13
Cake Artistry Centre
109 Midhurst Road. 020 8567 1081

car seats & accessories

Autosafe
PO Box 2923, W11 1ZB. 020 7221 9761

Motor Hoods
0800 163725
www.motorhoods.co.uk
Converts an estate into a seven-seater

cards for births & christenings

(see also birth announcements)

Announce It!
020 8286 4044
www.announceit.co.uk
See advert on page 17

Chatterbox Cards
PO Box 142, Beckenham, Kent BR3 6ZL.
020 8650 8650
www.chatterboxcards.com
See advert under birth announcements

Happy Hands
55 Sloane Square, Cliveden Place, SW1.
020 7730 5544
www.happyhands.ws
See advert on page 17

Heritage Personalised Stationery
01256 861738
www.heritage-stationery.com
See advert under birth announcements

c

● CARS ● MINIBUSES ●
● WELFARE VEHICLES ● COACHES ●

SEATBELT SPECIALISTS (SUPPLIERS & FITTERS)
● MOBILE FITTING SERVICE ●

CENTRE BELT

PHONE US ....
We can advise you on the correct products for your needs

020 7221 9761
MON-SAT

castings

Casts, usually of hands or feet, preserved in bronze, glass or on ceramic tiles.

First Impressions
263 Nether Street, N3. 020 8343 2453
www.judywiseman.com

Golden Hands, Silver Feet Ltd
Unit G, Homesdale Centre,
216-218 Homesdale Road, Bromley, Kent.
020 8290 4091
www.goldenhands.co.uk

Hands & Feet
020 8995 3638

Imprints
1 Brierley Road, SW12. 020 8772 0070

Sarah Page Sculpture
1 Frere Street, SW11. 020 7207 0884
www.sarahpagesculpture.co.uk

Wrightson & Platt
020 7652 2182
Bronze hands & feet

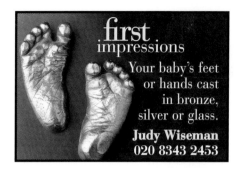

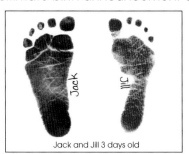

cassettes & cds

Cover to Cover Cassettes
PO Box 112, Marlborough, Wiltshire.
01672 562255
www.covertocover.co.uk

Cavalcade Story Cassettes
Chivers Press Ltd, Windsor Bridge Road,
Bath, BA2 3AX. 01225 335336

Nursery Stars
01273 300116
'Over The Moon', CD featuring favourite
nursery rhymes and lullabies

www.akilo.com
Baby language tapes to develop good
pronunciation. 24 languages

chemists, late opening

In case of emergency, police stations should
have information on local chemists which
may stay open late. The chemists listed
below stay open until midnight.

NW6
Bliss Chemists
50-56 Willesden Lane. 020 7624 8000

NW11
Warman Free Pharmacy
45 Golders Green Road. 020 8455 4351

SW5
Zafash Pharmacy
233-235 Old Brompton Road. 020 7373 3506

W1
Bliss Chemists
5-6 Marble Arch. 020 7723 6116

W4
Woolworth
356-362 Chiswick High Road. 020 8994 2025

chess

Richmond Junior Chess Club
020 8898 0362
richard@chesskids.com
6yrs+

childcare listings

Simply Childcare
16 Bushey Hill Road, SE5 8QJ.
020 7701 6111
www.simplychildcare.com

www.bestbear.co.uk

childminders

*(see also au pair agencies, babysitters, nanny
agencies)*

For lists of registered childminders in your
area, contact your local social services
department *(see councils).*

www.childminder.com

Please say you saw the ad in
The London Baby Directory

children's savings

(see also financial advice)

Tunbridge Wells Equitable Friendly Society
Abbey Court, St John's Road,
Tunbridge Wells, Kent.
0800 138 1381
www.babybond.co.uk
Baby Bond savings plan for children

For your free Baby Bond® information pack and Guide to Children's Savings visit:

www.babybond.co.uk

or call **0800 138 1381** quoting reference **BD1**

Baby Bond® is a registered service mark of Tunbridge Wells Equitable Friendly Society Ltd. Regulated by the Personal Investment Authority.

christening gifts & gowns

Baby List Company
The Broomhouse, 50 Sulivan Road, SW6.
020 7371 5145
See advert on page 149

Linen Merchant
11 Montpelier Street, SW7.
020 7584 3654

Christening Gowns
01536 515401
www.christeningoutfits.co.uk

Clair de Lune
0161 283 4476

First Occasion Ltd
023 9246 8810
firstoccasion@ukonline.co.uk

Little Angels
01604 582664
www.littleangels.co.uk

C

chiropractic

Suitable for treating back and neck pain.
May be useful for colic in babies.

British Chiropractic Association
0118 950 5950

McTimoney Chiropractic Association
21 High Street, Eynsham, Oxfordshire.
01865 880974
www.mctimoney-chiropractic.org

NW11/SW6
Dr Garry Russell
C/o Healthcare Chiropractic Clinic
020 7503 1383

cinemas

Many cinemas have a Saturday morning junior screening.

Barbican Centre
Silk Street, EC2. 020 7382 7000

Clapham Picture House
76 Venn Street, SW4. 020 7734 4342
Matinees for mothers with babies

Junior NFT
National Film Theatre, South Bank, SE1.
020 7928 3232

circumcision

Dr Leslie Solomon
16 Renters Avenue, Hendon, NW4.
020 8202 7760
lsolomon@aish.org.uk
Registered member of Initiation Society

Visit us at
www.babydirectory.com

Page 20 The London Baby Directory

c

Home Cleaning from

SELECTED CLEANERS
TO CLEAN AND CARE FOR YOUR HOME

Do you need someone locally to help with the cleaning and ironing?

How do you guarantee reliability? Someone honest, local & suitable? Would you like to have the same person each week?

1. As few as 2 hrs/wk, or as many as you need. You choose.
2. Screening, selection & vetting of workers.
3. All workers have written references.
4. Hourly rate FROM £6.75/hr.
5. Insurance for damage is included.
6. Travel to & from your house included.

Call **020 8968 4013**
Office Open 10.00am -8.00pm.

circus workshops

Circus Space
Coronet Street, N1.
020 7613 4141

Clowning Workshops
01342 82341

cleaners

Selclene Ltd
112 Portnall Road, Maida Vale, W9.
020 8968 4013

Myhome
London House,
42 Upper Richmond Road West, SW14.
0845 606 7080

SW
Simply Domestics
65 Colney Hatch Lane, N10.
020 8444 4304

clinics

Staffed by health visitors and community doctors, clinics provide health and development checks and are a good source of information and supplementary health care (e.g. family planning, chiropody, eye checks).

More information on-line

clothing shops

(see also mail order:clothing, maternity wear, nearly new shops, nursery goods, shoe shops)

We have not listed the major chains, e.g. Adams, Baby Gap, Boots, Hennes, Jigsaw Junior, John Lewis, Marks & Spencer, Monsoon, Mothercare, Next, etc, which can be found in most high streets.

E1
Kool Kids
9-11 New Goulston Street. 020 7247 2878

E3
Tiddlywinks
414 Roman Road. 020 8981 7000

EC1
Debbie Bliss
365 St John's Street. 020 7833 8255
www.debbiebliss.freeserve.co.uk

N1
Gotham Angels
23 Islington Green. 020 7359 8090

Jakss
319 Upper Street. 020 7359 4942

Baby Munchkins
186 Hoxton Street. 020 7684 5994

Trendys
72 Chapel Market. 020 7837 9070

Tiddlywinks
84 Chapel Market. 020 7278 5800

Kids Boutique
14 Chapel Market. 020 7837 4889

N8
Hobby Horse Riders
50-52 Crouch End Hill. 020 8348 9782

Snazzy Kids
30 Topsfield Parade, Tottenham Lane.
020 8348 5700

Gooseberry Bush
15 Park Road. 020 8342 9898
gberrybush@aol.com
See advert under maternity wear

N9
Precious One
Unit 36, 37-43 South Mall. 020 8807 5933

N10
Early Clothing
79-85 Fortis Green Road. 020 8444 9309

N12
Spoilt Brats
692 High Street.. 020 8445 2505

N16
Kiddie Chic
19 Amhurst Parade, Stamford Hill.
020 8880 1500

Shoe and Fashion Boutique
28 Stamford Hill. 020 8806 5581

NW3
Humla
9 Flask Walk. 020 7794 8449

NW6
Ranch
56 Salusbury Road. 020 7604 3300

NW8
Charly's
71 Church Street. 020 7723 6811

Tiddlywinks
23 St Johns Wood High Street.
020 7722 3033

NW10
Unipat Niles
132 High Road, Willesden. 020 8459 8189

NW11
Adam & Eve Children's Boutique
5 The Market Place, Hampstead Garden
Suburb. 020 8455 8645

Daphne & Mum
7 Belmont Parade, 838 Finchley Road.
020 8458 7095

Dynasty
1-2 Russell Parade, Golders Green Road.
020 8731 8521

SE10
Little Nippers
Plaza Arcade, 133 Vanburgh Hill,
Greenwich. 020 8293 4444

Me Childrenswear
5 Greenwich Market. 020 8858 6160

SE12
Twizzletots
4 Bridgefield Road

Traditional Clothing for Children from Birth to Seven Years

Young England Ltd, 47 Elizabeth Street, London SW1W 9PP
Tel: 020 7259 9003 Fax: 020 7730 5764
www.youngengland.com

clothing shops (cont.)

SE13
Matalan
Thurston Road, Loampit Lane.
020 8463 9830

Peacocks
143-149 High Street, Lewisham.
020 8852 0851

SE17
Peppermint for Kids
321-323 Walworth Road. 020 7703 9638

SE21
Biff
43 Dulwich Village. 020 8299 0911

SE26
Wearabouts
99 Sydenham Road. 020 8659 9917

SW1
Young England
47 Elizabeth Street. 020 7259 9003
www.youngengland.com

Bonpoint
35b Sloane Street. 020 7235 1441

Children's Pavilion
7 Pavilion Road. 020 7235 6513

Gucci
17-18 Sloane Street. 020 7235 6707

Oilily
9 Sloane Street. 020 7823 2505

Rachel Riley
14 Pont Street. 020 7259 5969
www.rachelriley.com

Semmalina
225 Ebury Street. 020 7730 9333

SW3
Miki House UK Ltd
107 Walton Street. 020 7838 0006

Agnes b
111 Fulham Road. 020 7225 3477

Butterscotch
172 Walton Street. 020 7581 8551

Daisy & Tom
181 King's Road. 020 7352 5000

French Connection Junior
140-144 Kings Road. 020 7225 3302

Joanna's Tent
289b Kings Road. 020 7352 1151

Patrizia Wigan Designs
19 Walton Street. 020 7823 7080

Trotters
34 Kings Road. 020 7259 9620

SW6
Baby List Company
The Broomhouse, 50 Sulivan Road.
020 7371 5145
See advert under nursery advisory service

Kent & Carey
154 Wandsworth Bridge Road.
020 7736 5554

Pollyanna
811 Fulham Road.

SW9
Great for Tomorrow
80 Atlantic Road. 020 7737 5276

SW11
Quackers
155d Northcote Road. 020 7978 4235

Stock House
155 Lavender Hill. 020 7738 0293

SW13
Bug Circus
153 Church Road. 020 8741 4244
www.kidsnclothes.co.uk

Membery's
1 Church Road. 020 8876 2910

Patrizia Wigan
61 Barnes High Street. 020 8876 4540

SW17
Smartees
5 Bellevue Parade, Wiseton Road.
020 8672 3392

SW19
Barney's Children's Store
6 Church Road. 020 8944 2915

clothing shops (cont.)

Children's Kingdom
209 Upper Tooting Road. 020 8682 2233

Gymboree
120 Centre Court, Wimbledon.
020 8879 3001

W1
Catimini
52 South Molton Street. 020 7629 8099

Gymboree
198 Regent's Street. 020 7494 1110

Humla
23 St Christopher's Place. 020 7224 1773

Minors
11 New Cavendish Street. 020 7486 8299

Polo Ralph Lauren
143 New Bond Street.

Tartine et Chocolat
66 South Molton Street. 020 7629 7233

Tommy Hilfiger
51 New Bond Street. 020 7290 9888
www.hilfiger.com

White House
51-52 New Bond Street. 020 7629 3521

W2
Bill Amberg
10 Chepstow Road, W2 5BD. 020 7727 3560
mail@billambergshop.demon.co.uk

W3
Trendy Tots
106 Churchfield Road. 020 993 7340

W4
Tots in the Terrace
39 Turnham Green Terrace. 020 8995 0520

W5
Juniper
88 Pitshanger Lane. 020 8998 0144

W8
Anthea Moore Ede
16 Victoria Grove. 020 7584 8826

Bonpoint Naissance
17 Victoria Grove. 020 7584 5131

Trotters
127 Kensington High Street. 020 7937 9373

What Katy Did...
49 Kensington Church Street. 020 7937 6499
kate@whatkatydid.free-online.co.uk

W10
Sasti
8 Portobello Green Arcade,
281 Portobello Road. 020 8960 1125

W11
Cath Kidston
8 Clarendon Cross. 020 7221 4000

The Cross
141 Portland Road. 020 7727 6760
www.thecrosscatalogue.com

WC2
Paul Smith for Children
44 Floral Street. 020 7379 7133
www.paulsmith.co.uk

Continental Childrens Clothing
for
babies, boys & girls

39 Turnham Green Terrace,
Chiswick W4 1RG
020 8995 0520

clubs

Scout Association
020 7584 7031
www.scoutbase.org.uk
Beavers from 6yrs, Cubs from 8yrs

Guide Association
020 7834 6242
www.guides.org.uk
Rainbows 5-7yrs, Brownies 8-12yrs

Kumon Educational
0800 854 714
www.kumon.c.uk *See advert on page 92*

colour analysis

Mirror Image
020 8992 8399
Colour & Style Analysis for you & your
Wardrobe

complementary health

*(see also acupuncture, aromatherapy,
homoeopathy, massage, osteopathy, reflexology,
yoga)*

Association of Systemic Kinesiology
020 8399 3215

Little Miracles
PO Box 3896, London NW3 7DS.
020 7431 6153
www.littlemiracles.co.uk
Flower essences - gentle remedies

C

complementary health (cont.)

Institute for Complementary Medicine
PO Box 194, London SE16 1QZ
Send sae for list of local addresses

National Institute of Medical Herbalists
01392 426022

mail order:

www.beamingbaby.com
0800 0345 672
Natural & Organic Products for Mother & Baby
See advert under nappies

www.Zitawest.com
08701 668899
See advert on page 154

centres:

N9
Keats Complementary Practice
1a Hydefield Court.
020 8803 2800

N10
Muswell Healing Arts
169 Avenue Mews.
020 8365 3545

N16
Clissold Park Natural Health Centre
154 Stoke Newington Church Street.
020 7249 2990

NW1
Neal's Yard Remedies
68 Chalk Farm Road. 020 7284 2039

Women and Health
4 Carol Street. 020 7482 2786

NW2
Chatsworth Clinic
4 Chatsworth Road. 020 8451 4754

NW8
Viveka
27a Queen's Terrace. 020 7483 0099

SE22
Family Natural Health Centre
106 Lordship Lane, East Dulwich.
020 8693 5515
www.soupdragon.co.uk

Vale Practice
64 Grove Vale. 020 8299 9798
www.thevalepractice.co.uk

SE23
The Karuna Healing Centre
103 Dartmouth Road, Forest Hill.
020 8699 4046

SE26
Newlands Park Natural Health Care Centre
48 Newlands Park, Sydenham.
020 8659 5001

SW2
Awareness in Pregnancy
79 Brixton Hill. 020 8671 5390
Guidance to tune into your needs and the baby

SW3
Neal's Yard Remedies
Chelsea Farmers Market, Sydney Street.
020 7351 6380

SW4
South London Natural Health Centre
7a Clapham Common Southside.
020 7720 8817

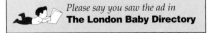

SW15
Putney Natural Therapy Clinic
11 Montserrat Road. 020 8789 2548

SW17
The Art of Health & Yoga Centre
280 Balham High Road. 020 8682 1800

SW20
Living Centre Clinic
32 Durham Road, Raynes Park.
020 8946 2331

W1
Awareness in Pregnancy
c/o Nature Works, 16 Balderton Street.
020 8671 5390
Guidance to tune into your needs and the baby

Harley Street Complementary Care
1 Harley Street. 0870 241 4025
www.complementary-care.co.uk

Natureworks
16 Balderton Street. 020 7355 4036

W4
Equilibrium
150 Chiswick High Road. 020 8742 7701

W5
Oaktrees Clinic
31 The Mall. 020 8566 2920

W6
Craven Clinic
54 Cambridge Grove. 020 8563 8133

Mellennium Clinic
Richford Gate Primary Care Centre,
Richford Street. 020 8846 7539
www.mellenniumclinic.co.uk

Visit us at
www.babydirectory.com

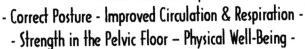

complementary health (cont.)

W8
Life Centre
15 Edge Street. 020 7221 4602

The Grove Health Centre
182-184 Kensington Church Street.
020 7221 2266

W11
Neal's Yard Remedies
9 Elgin Crescent. 020 7727 3998

W12
BushMaster Natural Health Practice
204 Uxbridge Road. 020 8749 3792

WC2
Neal's Yard Remedies
15 Neal's Yard, Covent Garden.
020 7379 7222

computers for children

Click On
020 8446 1310

Computer Workshops
SW11. 020 7585 2067

TechnoKids
020 7354 9678

concerts

West London Sinfonia
020 8997 3540
Big concert every Christmas

Barbican
Silk Street, EC2. 020 7638 8891
LSO Family Concerts

English Heritage Musical Summer Evenings
020 7973 3427
Concerts at Kenwood, Marble Hill House

Visit us at
www.babydirectory.com

cookery

c

Dodo Cookbook
PO Box 10507, London N22 7WZ.
0870900 8004
www.dodopad.com
See advert under gifts

NW11
Gill's Cookery Workshop
10 Sutcliffe Close. 020 8458 2608
6yrs+

SW4
Fix A Feast
17 Narbonne Avenue. 020 8675 9657

SW8
Cookie Crumbles
10-14 Southville. 020 7622 4448
jane@cookiecrumbles.fsnet.co.uk
5-16yrs

W1
Les Petits Cordons Bleus
114 Marylebone Lane. 020 7935 3503
www.cordonbleu.net
7yrs+

W3
Kids' Cookery School
107 Gunnersbury Lane. 020 8932 5837
3-18yrs

W11
Books for Cooks Workshop
4 Blenheim Crescent. 020 7221 1992
info@booksforcooks.com

cord blood storage

Storage of small amount of blood from umbilical cord for potential use for treatment for the child later in life.

UK Cord Blood Bank
7 Crossway, Chesham, Buckinghamshire.
01494 786117
www.cordbloodbank.co.uk

www.babydirectory.com

Haringey
childcare
Information
Service

Park Lane Family Learning Centre
139 Park Lane, Tottenham, N17 0HN
Fax: 020 8493 8863
Web site: www.childcarelink.gov.uk

020 8801 1234

councils

Your local council is an excellent source of information. Ask for the Under 8s section, Early Years' section, or leisure. They can provide lists of local nurseries, schools, parks, etc. Some produce excellent booklets on their area. Postcodes are approximate since some councils cover several areas.

E6
London Borough of Newham
020 8472 1430
Newham for Kids

E8
London Borough of Hackney
020 8356 5000
List of children's clubs, *Under Eights Guide*

E14
London Borough of Tower Hamlets
020 7364 5000

E17
Waltham Forest Council
020 8527 5544

EC2
Corporation of London
020 7606 3030

EN
London Borough of Barnet
020 8359 3029

HA9
London Borough of Brent
020 8937 1234

KT1
Royal Borough of Kingston upon Thames
020 8547 6582
Children's Information Service

N1
London Borough of Islington
Starting Out, £2.50. Under 5s information line (south): 020 7477 3516; (north) 020 7226 3553. Mon, Wed, Fri (3.15-4.45)

N22
London Borough of Haringey
020 8489 000
childcare: 020 8801 1234

NW1
London Borough of Camden
020 7278 4444
Cindex database available in libraries

NW4
London Borough of Barnet
020 8359 2000
Under Fives in Barnet, £1

SE5
London Borough of Southwark
020 7525 5000

SE6
London Borough of Lewisham
020 8314 6000
Early Years - The Directory of Services for Young Children in Lewisham

SE18
London Borough of Greenwich
020 8854 8888

SW1
City of Westminster
020 7641 6000
Under 8s Welcome Booklet

SW2
London Borough of Lambeth
020 7926 1000
Children's Play in Lambeth

SW16/SW19/SW20/CR4/SM4
London Borough of Merton
020 8543 2222
Under 8s guide

SW18
London Borough of Wandsworth
020 8871 6000

TW1
London Borough of Richmond upon Thames
020 8891 1411

W4/TW3
London Borough of Hounslow
020 8583 2000
www.hounslow.gov.uk
A-Z Guide for 0-12s

W5
London Borough of Ealing
020 8579 2424
Directory of Day Care & Related Services for Children under 8

W6
London Borough of Hammersmith & Fulham
020 8748 3020
information@inet.lbhf.gov.uk
Services for children under 8
See advert under sports

W8
Royal Borough of Kensington & Chelsea
020 7937 5464
Directory of Services for Children under Eight

cradles

(see also nursery furniture & décor)

Swingers & Rockers
Terfyn Uchaf, Rhiw,Pwllheli, Gwynedd.
01758 780305
www.cradles.co.uk

craniosacral therapy

(see also osteopathy)
Craniosacral Therapy Association
07000 784735
www.craniosacral.co.uk

c

crèches, mobile

Crêchendo
020 8772 8120

Mobile Crèche Company
01423 797440

cricket

Maurice Jules Cricket Courses
020 8969 1365
5yrs+. Football, sports parties, etc

cycling & cycling attachments

Living Lightly
0800 0745 332
Buggy carrier

Two plus two UK
31 Western Road, St Anne's, Lewes,
East Sussex. 01273 480479
www.twoplustwo.uk.com
Trailers, joggers, etc

Zero Emissions
020 7723 2409
www.workbike.org
Family trailers, Christiania Tricycle, etc

London Cycling Campaign
020 7928 7220
Campaigns for better facilities

Parks, Playgrounds and Pubs
020 8946 0912
Family rides

London Recumbents
East Carriage Drive, Battersea Park, SW11.
020 7498 6543
Fun bike rental

dance

(see also art, drama, gym, music)

Dance teachers tend to hold classes in different venues within a general area, so check neighbouring postcodes, as the teacher may be listed there. Most ballet classes are for children from 3 years upwards unless otherwise stated.

Dalcroze Society
020 8645 0714
Music education through movement

Imperial Society of Teachers of Dancing
22-26 Paul Street, EC2A 4QE. 020 7377 1577
Send A4 sae for list saying which type of dance for 5yrs+

International Dance Teachers' Association Ltd
01273 685 652
Ring for a list of teachers in your area

Dalcroze Society
020 8645 0714
Music education through movement

International Dance Teachers' Association Ltd
International House, 76 Bennett Road, Brighton BN2 5JL. 01273 685 652
Ring for a list of teachers in your area

E3
Chisenhale Dance Space
64-84 Chisenhale Road, E3. 020 8981 6617

E11
Chantraine School of Dance
020 8989 8604

E15
East London Dance
Old Town Hall, 29 The Broadway, E15.
020 8519 2200
Contact for details of other classes in the area

EC1
Central School of Ballet
10 Herbal Hill, Clerkenwell Road, EC1.
020 7837 6332
4-12yrs

N1
City Dance Academy
020 7359 2273

Islington Ballet School
020 7226 5444

N5
Highbury Roundhouse
71 Ronalds Road. 020 7359 5916

N6
Lauderdale House
Waterlow Park, Highgate Hill.
020 8348 8716

BabyMoves
78 Highgate West Hill. 020 8348 3752
sukigram@dircon.co.uk
3-20mths

N7
Islington Arts Factory
2 Parkhurst Road. 020 7607 0561
6yrs+

N10
Crazee Kids
c/o Cornerways, Ellington Road.
020 8444 5333

North London School of Performing Arts
76 St James Lane. 020 8444 4544
5-18yrs

N19
Lucy Harmer School of Dance
Highgate Newtown Community Centre,
25 Bertram Street. 020 7272 7201
hncc@camvolsec12.demon.co.uk

N20
Finchley Ballet School
109 Greenway. 020 8445 3387

N22
Alexandra Palace
Alexandra Palace Way, Wood Green.
020 8365 2121

Sandra Pepper School of Dancing
020 8888 2955
3yrs+

NW1
Marylebone Ballet School
01992 813650

NW1
Ready, Steady, Go
020 7586 5862

NW1/NW3
Hampstead Dance Theatre Group
Primrose Hill Community Centre,
29 Hopkinson's Place. 020 8908 0505

Chalk Farm School of Dance
020 8348 0262

Biodanza
020 7485 2369
5yrs+

NW3
Stella Mann School of Dancing
020 7435 9317

NW6
Abbey Community Centre
222C Belsize Road, NW6 4DJ. 020 7435 4247
4-7yrs. Also drama

NW8
St John's Wood Ballet School
01992 813650

SE
Pippa Hurrell Ballet Tap and Modern
020 8249 2915

The Marylebone Ballet School
St. John's Wood Ballet School
Children's ballet classes and exams taken in
The Cecchetti Method
(The Imperial Society of Teachers of Dancing)
Also creative dance for Children from 3 years.
For further information or brochure please phone
Belinda Payne A.I.S.T.D. (Dip)
01992 813650

SE5
Donald McAlpine Dance Studio
Longfield Hall, 50 Knatchbull Road.
020 8673 4992

SE10
Greenwich Dance Agency
The Borough Hall, Royal Hill.
020 8293 9741
0-18yrs

SE14
Laban Centre
Laurie Grove. 020 8692 4070

SE21/SE27
Nightingale Dance Studios
020 8761 7901
2^1/2-16yrs

SE22
Campbell School of Stage Dance
020 8768 0782

SE22/SE27
Beryl Low School of Dance
020 8244 9185
3yrs+

SW1
Chelsea Ballet School
020 7351 4117

Westminster School of Dancing
020 7828 0651

Visit us at
www.babydirectory.com

dance (cont.)

SW1/SW11/SW12
Vacani School of Dancing
020 7592 9255
Also at Belgravia, Clapham, Fulham,
Bayswater, Richmond, East Sheen

SW1
Westminster School of Performing Art
St Andrews Club, 12 Old Pye Street.
020 7222 8873
Drama, singing. Kicks for Kids

SW3/SW7
La Sylvaine School
020 8964 0561

SW4
Spring School of Ballet
The Contact Centre, Hambalt Road.
01276 709393
$2^1/_2$yrs+

SW6
First Steps Ballet
020 7381 5224

Wendy Bell School of Dance and Fitness
020 7371 9652
$2^1/_2$yrs+

SW7
West London School of Dancing
020 8743 3856

SW10
Childsplay
Ashburnham Community Centre,
Upcerne Road. 020 7727 9307

SW11
Sam Hawkins School of Dance
020 8847 3792

Royal Academy of Dancing
36 Battersea Square. 020 7223 0091
www.rad.org.uk
Can provide lists. 3yrs+

SW11/SW12/SW17/SW18
Rainbow School of Ballet
020 8877 0703

SW12
Kaleidoscope School of Performing Arts
Balham Studio, 21 Ramsden Road.
020 8715 5076
$3^1/_2$yrs+

SW12/SW17/SW18/SW19
Southfields School of Ballet
020 7737 5033
$2^1/_2$yrs+

SW13
Woolborough Academy
Woolborough House, 39 Lonsdale Road.
020 8351 7713
3yrs+

SW13/SW15/W6/W8
Southwest School of Ballet
020 8392 9565

SW13/W4/W6
London Dance School
020 8940 3793

SW14
Studioflex
26 Priests Bridge. 020 8878 0556

SW16
ABC Ballet School
St James Church Hall, Welham Road.
020 8769 4337

Streatham School of Dance
020 8857 4206

SW17
Jean Winkler's Dance Studio
261 Burntwood Lane,
Wandsworth Common. 020 8874 2142
Music & movement, ballet

SW17/SW19
Village Dancing School
020 8543 1394

SW19
Cherry Dunn Dancing Classes
St John's Church Hall, Spencer Hill.
020 8946 1523
2^{1}/$_{2}$-17yrs

Dance Club
St Luke's Church Hall, Strathmore Road,
Wimbledon Park. 020 8679 3040

SW20
Footsteps School of Dance and Drama
020 8540 3090

W1/W11
West London School of Dancing
020 8743 3856

W4
Arts Educational Schools
14 Bath Road, W4 1LY. 020 8987 6666

W4/W12
Frances Lundy School of Dance
020 8675 0433

W5
June Carlyle School of Educational Dance
Ascension Church Hall, Beaufort Road.
020 8992 4122
3yrs+. Ballet, tap, etc

Margaret Dance Academy
Pitshanger Methodist Church,
Pitshanger Lane. 020 8740 0727

Pirouette
Questors Theatre, Mattock Lane.
020 8840 5122

Ruth Barber
Ellen Wilkinson High School,
Queens Drive. 01923 820941
ballet, 3yrs+

Ealing Dance Centre
96 Pitshanger Lane. 020 8998 2283
3yrs+. Also dance shop
www.ealingdance.co.uk

Ealing YMCA
St Mary's Road. 020 8799 4800

W7
Crackerjack
99 Oaklands Road. 020 8840 3355

W10
Tiddleywinks
Wornington Road. 020 7573 5328
2-3yrs

d

Bramley's Dance Classes
Bramley's Big Adventure,
136 Bramley Road. 020 8960 1515

W11
Portobello School of Ballet
59A Portobello Road. 020 8969 4125

The Tabernacle
Powis Square. 020 7435 8217
Performing arts and sports

WC1
The Place
17 Dukes Road. 020 7388 8430
5yrs+

Bedford House Community Centre
35 Emerald Street. 020 7405 2370

WC2
Pineapple Dance Studios
7 Langley Street. 020 7836 4004

Susan Zalcman School of Ballet
Pineapple Studios, 7 Langley Street.
020 7289 1869

Local events & news

d

Gentle Dental Care
For Health and Confidence

Lady Dentist Devoted to Care
Of the Highest Quality

Treatment for
Children of All Ages
and
Nervous Patient Programme

Dr Issi Mahmood BDS HONS (LONDON)
Private Practice - 100 Harley Street
London W1N 1AF
www.100harleyst.co.uk
email info@100harleyst.co.uk

020 7935 3668/6100

01795 428150

complete

creative

solutions

Design & print

E-mail: sioux.lbgraphics@cableinet.co.uk

lb graphics

dentists

N2
Total Dental Care
240 East End Road. 020 8905 5900

N12
Gentle Dental Care
21 Woodhouse Road, North Finchley.
020 8445 2114

W1
Gentle Dental Care
100 Harley Street, W1. 020 7935 3668
www.100harleyst.co.uk

Dr Malcolm Levinkind
Suite 6, 103-5 Harley Street. 020 8444 3413

Dentistry for Children
33 Weymouth Street. 020 7580 5370

department stores

John Lewis Brent Cross
Brent Cross Shopping Centre, NW4.
020 8202 6535

Peter Jones
Sloane Square, SW1. 020 7730 3434

John Lewis
Oxford Street, W1. 020 7629 7711

depressed

Cheer up!!

design

LB Graphics
01795 428150
sioux.lbgraphics@cableinet.co.uk
Small business specialists
LB Graphics would especially like to thank
Hannah Levy for all her effort and hard work

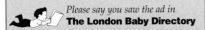
Please say you saw the ad in
The London Baby Directory

designer outlets

Amazon
22 Kensington Church Street, W8.
020 7937 4692

Bicester Village
Bicester, Oxfordshire. 01869 323200

French Connection Factory Shop
3 Hancock Road, Bromley-by-Bow, E3.
020 7399 7125
6yr-olds only

Great Western Designer Outlet
Kemble Drive, Swindon. 01793 507600
www.macarthurglen.com
Junction 16, M4

dolls' houses

Ealing Miniatures
020 8998 7990

Little Wonders
3 York Street, Twickenham TW1
020 8255 6114
See advert under toy shops

Raymond Luke
020 8384 6962
Forts, farms

Singing Tree
69 New King's Road, SW6. 020 7736 4527

doulas

A doula provides physical, emotional and
practical support for the family during
pregnancy, labour and immediately after
the birth.

Clare Benson
020 8673 4439

Hilary Lewin
01306 730796

Liz Murray
020 8874 5184

Millennia Doulas
020 7722 4786
Training and supply

Mothers' Care Doulas
020 7209 2231
motherscaredoulas@handbag.com

d

Heather Guerrini
020 7352 0245
Training courses

**Tinies International & Central
London**
351 Fulham Palace Road, SW6.
020 7384 0322
www.tinieschildcare.co.uk
See advert under nannies.

Top Notch Nannies
49 Harrington Gardens, SW7.
020 7259 2626
See advert under nannies

drama

*(see also art, dance, gym, music and theatres
which often run drama courses)*

Greasepaint Anonymous
020 8886 2263
4yrs+

Stagecoach HQ
01932 254333
www.stagecoach.co.uk
Ring for details of your local area

E1
**Pollyanna Children's Training
Theatre**
Metropolitan Wharf, Wapping Wall.
020 7702 1937
3-20yrs

drama (cont.)

North
Helen O'Grady Drama Academy
020 7609 5577

N1
Speech & Drama Workshops
01202 681829

N1/NW1
Perform
020 7209 3805
www.perform.org.uk

N5
Hot Tin Roof Drama Project
Highbury Round House, Donalds Road.
020 8858 7324
4yrs+

N6
Stage Coach
020 8361 8999

N10
North London Performing Arts Centre
76 St James Lane. 020 8444 4544

NW3
Dramarama
South Hampstead High School, Maresfield Gardens. 020 8446 0891

NW3/SW5
Allsorts
020 8969 3249
3-16yrs

NW6
Tricycle Theatre
269 Kilburn High Road. 020 7328 1000

NW11
Club Dramatika
020 8883 1554

South
Helen O'Grady Drama Academy
020 8239 0053

SE
Helen O'Grady Drama Academy
020 8880 6494

O'Farrell Stage School
020 8333 0080
4-16yrs

SE3
Blackheath Conservatoire of Music and the Arts
19-21 Lee Road. 020 8852 0234

SE5
Stagecoach
020 7738 6422

New Peckham Varieties
Havil Street. 020 7708 5401
4yrs+

SE16/SW19
Drama Club
020 7231 6083
samantha.giblin@tesco.net
5yrs+

SE22
Bright Sparks Theatre School
Dulwich Constitutional Club,
33 East Dulwich Grove. 020 8769 3500

James Allen's Saturday Centre for Performing Arts
020 8693 6021
7-14yrs

SW11
Rise Theatre Arts School
020 7924 1404
4-16yrs

SW13/SW14/W4/W6
Helen O'Grady's Drama Academy
020 8894 0804
5yrs+

SW19
Polka Theatre
240 The Broadway. 020 8543 4888
www.polkatheatre.com

W3
Barbara Speake Stage School
East Acton Lane. 020 8743 1306

W4
Arts Educational Schools
14 Bath Road. 020 8987 6666

W6
Drama at Tea Time
St Peter's Church, St Peter's Square.
020 8995 0664
2-7yrs

educational consultants

(see also helplines: education, schools, tuition)

Gabbitas Educational Consultants
Carrington House, 126-130 Regent Street,
W1. 020 7734 0161
www.gabbitas.com
See advert under schools

ISIS London & South-East
Grosvenor Gardens House,
35-37 Grosvenor Gardens, SW1.
020 7798 1560
southeast@isis.org.uk
www.isis.org.uk/southeast
See advert under schools

elephant training

Not recommended for under 5 years

exercise classes for ante- and post-natal

(see also antenatal support & information, health clubs with creches, personal trainers, swimming pools, yoga)

Local leisure centres and maternity hospitals often hold exercise classes for new mothers.

London Academy of Personal Fitness
0870 442 3231
www.lapf.co.uk

Guild of Postnatal Exercise Teachers
01453 884268
www.postnatalexercise.co.uk

Momentum Fitness
020 8772 1346

Association of Personal Trainers
020 7836 1102

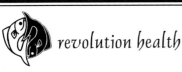

revolution health

Personal Training
for Mums and 'Mums to Be'

Get *(back)* in Shape
and Stay in Shape

Exercise boosts energy levels!

All fitness requirements catered for.
Pre and Post Natal Exercise Programmes.
General Fitness Schedules.
At Home, in the Gym or in the Park.
Also available:
Nutrition Advice and Programmes
Relaxation and Flexibility

Call Karen for a Consultation

0958 464770

N/NW/W and Central London Only

exercise classes for ante- and post-natal (cont.)

Revolution Health
020 7289 4111

Bodyback
020 8673 0030

N2
Fit for 2
020 8931 2085
Also Pilates

N7
Fit Start
Sobell Leisure Centre, Hornsey Road.
020 8374 7680

N10
Susana Weiner
020 8444 4284

NW1
Fit Start
Mornington Sports Centre. 020 8374 7680

SW1
Fit Mums, Happy Kids
Dolphin Square Sports Centre,
Chichester Street.
020 7798 8686
www.dolphinsquare.co.uk
Swimming pool

SW16
Ante Natal Exercise
020 8769 3613
Also antenatal teacher

SW17
Rosemary Kennett
125 Drakefield Road. 020 8767 4560

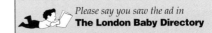

West
Gillian Leslie
020 8992 8399

W4
Rosemary Newman Postnatal Shape Up Classes
44 Hartington Road. 020 8994 0369
rosemary_newman@hotmail.com

W7
Crackerjack
99 Oaklands Road. 020 8840 3355

W8
The Life Centre
15 Edge Street. 020 7221 4602
See advert under complementary health

Para Normal Mum

ex-pat advice

American Women's Club of London
68 Old Brompton Road, SW7.
london.fawco.org

Focus Information Services
13 Prince of Wales Terrace, W8.
020 7937 0050

Person Allies
29 Flat C, Whittingstall Road, SW6.
020 7371 9483

Normal Mum

Reproduced by kind permission of **The Dodo Pad**©
"The perfect antidote to organisational chaos".
See advertisement under Gifts

We can often help

On Springs

family planning

Contact the organisations listed below for details of your nearest centre.
For sex after giving birth, *see page 338*

British Pregnancy Advisory Service (BPAS)
26 Bedford Square, WC1. 020 7637 8962

Brook Advisory Centre
020 7580 2991
Free advice and treatment

Family Planning Association
020 7837 4044

Marie Stopes House
020 7388 0662

Off Springs

fancy dress

mail order:

Charlie Crow
01782 417133

Fairytales
PO Box 21220, London W9 1ZE.
020 7286 7142

Hopscotch
61 Palace Road, London SW2. 0208 674 9853
www.hopscotchmailorder.co.uk

Little Wings
020 7243 3840
www.littlewings.co.uk

retail:

N2
Culture Vultures Ltd
200 High Road, East Finchley. 020 8883 5525

NW1
Escapade
150 Camden High Street. 020 7485 7384
escapade@dircon.co.uk
5yrs+

SW10
Fancy That! Ltd
92 Lots Road. 020 7351 7291

W10
The Fan Club
The Old Dairy, 133 Kilburn Lane.
020 8932 1313
www.thefanclub.co.uk

farms: city farm

(see also farms: out of town, nature reserves, outings, zoos)

E1
Stepping Stones Farm
Stepney Way / Stepney High Street.
020 7790 8204
Closed Mondays

Spitalfields Farm Association
Weaver Street. 020 7247 8762

E2
Hackney City Farm
1a Goldsmiths Row, off Hackney Road.
020 7729 6381
Closed Mondays

E10
Brooks Farm
Skeltons Lane Park, Leyton. 020 8539 4278
Closed Mondays, except Bank Holidays

E14
Mudchute Farm
Pier Street, Isle of Dogs. 020 7515 5901

E16
Newham City Farm
King George Avenue. 020 7476 1170
Closed Monday

N3
College Farm
45 Fitzalan Road. 020 8349 0690

N7
Freightliners Farm
Sheringham Road. 020 7609 0467

NW5
Kentish Town City Farm
1 Cressfield Close. 020 7916 5421
Pony club

SE11
Vauxhall City Farm
24 St Oswalds Place. 020 7582 4204

SE16
Surrey Docks City Farm
Rotherhithe Street. 020 7231 1010

SW19
Deen City Farm
39 Windsor Avenue, Merton Abbey.
020 8543 5300
deencity@deencityfarm.co.uk
Also riding

WC1
Coram's Fields
93 Guilford Street. 020 7837 6138
Seven acres with pets' corner, pigs, guinea
pigs

farms: out of town

(see also farms: city, nature reserves, outings, zoos)

■ *Buckinghamshire*
Odds Farm Park
Wooburn Common, High Wycombe.
01628 520188
www.oddsfarm.co.uk
Off at Jct 2 of M40

■ *Essex*
Marsh Farm Country Park
South Woodham Ferrers. 01245 321552

■ *Hertfordshire*
Aldenham Country Park
Dagger Lane, Elstree. 020 8953 9602

Bowmans Open Farm & Falconry Centre
Coursers Road, London Colney, St Albans.
01727 822106

Longford Children's Farm
St Margaret's, Great Gaddesden,
Hemel Hempstead. 01442 843471

Wimpole Hall Home Farm
Arrington, Royston. 01223 207257

■ *Surrey*
Bocketts Farm Park
Young Street, Fetcham, nr Leatherhead.
01372363764

Burpham Court Farm Park
Clay Lane, Jacobs Well, Guildford.
01483 576089
A3 to Burpham and Merrow

Godstone Farm
Godstone. 01883 742546

Horton Park Children's Farm
Horton Lane, Epsom. 01372743984

Lockwood Donkey Sanctuary
Farm Cottage, Sanhills,
Wormley, nr Godalming. 01428 682409

fatherhood

This book is for you too, you know

DIY Dads
320 Commercial Way, SE15. 020 7732 9409

Families Need Fathers
134 Curtain Road, EC2. 020 7613 5060
www.fnf.org.uk

www.fathersdirect.com

feng shui

Feng Shui Partnership
020 8883 1261
fengshuipartnership@bigfoot.com
See advert under nursery furniture

financial advice

Aberdeen Unit Trust Managers
1 Bow Church Yard, London EC4.
020 7364 6000

Family Assurance Friendly Society
0800 616695

Friends Provident
United Kingdom House, 72-122 Castle
Street, Salisbury, Wiltshire. 01722 318000

IFG Life & Pensions Ltd
Indemnity House, Meadow Lane, St Ives,
Cambridgeshire. 0345 660559

Invesco Europe
11 Devonshire Square, London EC2.
020 7626 3434

Invest for School Fees
10 Trinity Square, London EC3.
020 7488 8336

John Charcol Ltd
0800 718191

Rebroke Limited
1st Floor, Victoria Buildings, Middlewich,
Cheshire CW10 9AT.
08000 852514
www.rebroke.com
See advert under life assurance

Royston Fox
Russell Fox Nori, 117 Piccadilly, Mayfair,
London W1V 9FJ. 020 7744 6556
royston.fox@sjpp.co.uk

**Tunbridge Wells Equitable Friendly
Society,**
Abbey Court, St John's Road,
Tunbridge Wells, Kent. 0800 138 1381
www.babybond.co.uk
Baby Bond savings plan for children
See advert under children's savings

first aid courses

Crêchendo Training
1 Grange Mills, Weir Road. 020 8772 8160
training@crechendo.com
www.crechendo.com

The Parent Company
6 Jacob's Well Mews, W1. 020 7935 0123
www.theparentcompany.co.uk

flower remedies

Little Miracles
PO Box 3896, London NW3 7DS.
020 7431 6153
www.littlemiracles.co.uk
Flower remedies.
See advert under complementary health

because children don't come with instructions!

Crêchendo runs a range of informative courses and seminars for parents. Our courses trainers are professionals and, as parents themselves, they have a realistic and refreshing approach.

Our current courses include:

- First Aid for Babies and Children
- Baby Massage
- Child Development Workshop
- Understanding your Child's Behaviour

For more details contact
Alice or Kate
020 8772 8160
training@crechendo.com
www.crechendo.com

food

■ *for baby*

Babynat
020 8340 0401
www.organico.co.uk

Baby Organix
0800 393511

Hipp
0800 448822

MiniMeals
07980 916496
minimeals@characin.co.uk
National delivery, frozen baby food

Portobello Food Company
020 8748 0505
www.portobellofood.com

■ *for grown ups*

Beth Pollock's Emergency Food Rescue Packs
020 7630 0695
Home-made food delivered for your first weeks at home after the birth

f

football

Football in the Community run weekend and holiday courses for 5yrs+.
(see also leisure centres)

Brentford
020 8758 9430

Charlton Athletic
020 8850 2866

Chelsea
020 7385 0710

Fulham
020 7893 8383

Leyton Orient
Leyton Community Sport Programme.
020 8556 5973

Milwall
The Den, Zempa Road. 020 7231 1222
9yrs+

Queens Park Rangers
020 8743 0262

West Ham United
Boleyn Ground, Green Street, Upton Park.
020 8548 2707
6yrs+

Pitz Five-a-Side Football Club
Bobby Moore Way, Friern Barnet, N10.
020 8442 1000
5yrs+

Kick It
01895 435571
3-12yrs

franchise opportunities

No Baby Directory in your area? Ring us on
020 8742 8724.

french

■ *Bookshops*

Librairie la Page
7 Harrington Road, SW7. 020 7589 5991

French Bookshop
28 Bute Street, SW7. 020 7584 2840

French Letters
135 Lower Richmeond Road. SW15
020 8785 7777

■ *Classes & clubs*

Bonjour French Fun
020 8670 7134

Les Chatons
020 7584 3964

Le club français
01962 714 036

Le club frère Jacques
020 7354 0589

Club Petit Pierrot
020 7828 2129

Le club tricolore
020 7924 4649

Conversation Piece
020 8579 4567
www.conversation-piece.co.uk

French à la carte
020 8946 4777

French Ecole
020 8858 4030
www.frenchecole.com
3-11yrs

French for Little Ones
020 7351 0608

La Jolie Ronde
020 8555 1358
info@lajolieronde.co.uk

Le Kinderclub
020 8943 5363

Les Petits Lapins
020 8947 0021

Les Petites Marionnettes
020 7637 5698

■ *Nannies*

Franglais Nannies
020 8646 7663
See advert under nanny agencies

■ *Nurseries*

NW5
L'ile aux enfants
22 Vicars Road. 020 7267 7119
3-11yrs

NW11
Pomme d'Api
86 Wildwood Road. 020 8455 1417
1-4yrs. mornings only

SE13
Diabolo Menthe
Kingswood Hall, Kingswood Place,
Blackheath. 020 8318 3067
Parent and toddler playgroup, 0-4yrs

SW12
L'Ecole des Benjamins
c/o Alderbrooke Primary School,
Oldridge Road. 020 8673 8525
ledblondon@aol.com
6 mths-7yrs. Full day

SW1
French Nursery School
77-79 Kinnerton Street. 020 7584 3964
2-5yrs

SW6
Ecole des Petits
2 Hazlebury Road. 020 7371 8350

W6
**Ecole Française de Londres: Jacques
Prévert**
59 Brook Green. 020 7602 6871
4-11yrs

Le Hérisson
The Methodist Church, Rivercourt Road.
020 8563 7664
2-6yrs

W10
Petite Ecole Française
90 Oxford Gardens. 020 8960 1278
21mths-6yrs

■ *Tapes*

Scarecrow
020 8567 7842
Also German

german classes, playgroups & schools

N1/N5
German Saturday School
020 7281 8167
Bilingual backgrounds only

N6
German Playgroup
020 8201 9179
020 8444 2290

South West
Le Kinderclub
020 8943 5363

SW1
German Parent and Toddler Group
020 7630 5940

SW6
German Club
020 7610 6954

TW9
German Saturday School
020 8942 5663

TW10
German School
Douglas House, Petersham Road,
Richmond. 020 8940 2510
5-18yrs

West
German Playgroup
020 8575 1816
Thursdays

W2
German Saturday School
020 7229 3740
3yrs+

W5
German Saturday School
020 8567 8381

gifts

(see also mail order)

Alice Hart & Company
020 8663 1248
www.alicehart.co.uk

Annie Haak Designs
01730 895558
www.anniehaak.co.uk

Astrological Baby Profiles
01724 761404
www.elysian.co.uk

Baby & Co.
020 7373 0574
www.babyandco.co.uk

Baby Gem
01932 863999
www.babygem.com

Baby Goody Boxes
020 8856 1100

www.beamingbaby.com
0800 0345 672
Natural & Organic Products for
Mother & Baby
See advert under nappies

Dodopad
PO Box 10507, London N22 7WZ.
0870 900 8004
www.dodopad.com

www.gifts4baby.co.uk
Box containing baby gifts of your choice
with personalised message

Goslings Gift Company
01386 701529
www.goslingsfungifts.com

International Star Registry
020 7226 6886

Kitty's Antique Prints & Maps
020 8992 5104
www.kittyprint.com

Sally Haigh Handpainted Designs
020 8995 7249

gifts (cont.)

Serena Harrison's Gifts for Godchildren
01249 821019

Storks Celebrations Ltd
0800 1694026

Stork Express
01494 434294
www.storkexpress.co.uk
See advert on page 49

■ *Local companies*

Anne Taylor Designs
020 8748 9279
www.anne-taylor.co.uk
Hand-painted photograph frames

Beverley Hills Bakery
020 7584 4401
Cake baby basket

Gillian Wood Ceramics
020 8995 3638

Hampers from Hampstead
020 7435 1847
hamp.ham@virgin.net

Happy Hands
55 Sloane Square, Cliveden Place.
020 7730 5544
www.happyhands.ws
Hand and foot prints and works of art
preserved on ceramic tiles.
See advert under cards

guardianship

Chosen Inheritance
Victoria House, 2 Victoria Terrace,
Ealing Green. 020 8840 4080
legal.services@onet.co.uk
www.choseninheritance.co.uk
See advert under wills

gym

(see also leisure centres)

Many local leisure centres offer gym
classes.

Crêchendo Playgyms
020 8772 8120
playgyms@crechendo.com
www.crechendo.com
Throughout London

Tumble Tots
0121 585 7003
Ring for your local contact

N1/N4
Bizzy Bodies
020 7713 1388

N7
Fit Start
Sobell Leisure Centre, Hornsey Road.
020 8374 7680
See advert under exercise

N8
Hornsey YMCA
184 Tottenham Lane. 020 8340 6088

N9
Lee Valley Leisure Centre
Picketts Lock Lane. 020 8345 6666

N19
Highgate Newtown Community Centre Skate and Bounce
25 Bertram Street. 020 7272 7201
hncc@camvolsec12.demon.co.uk

N22
Alexandra Palace
Alexandra Palace Way, Wood Green.
020 8365 2121

NW1
Fit Start
Mornington Sports Centre. 020 8374 7680
See advert under exercise

NW11
Tumbling Toddlers
The Institute, Central Square, Hampstead
Garden Suburb. 020 8455 9951
www.hgsi.ac.uk

SE1
Elite Rhythmic Gymnastics
Elephant & Castle Leisure Centre.
020 7252 5594

SE13
Ladywell Gym Club
The Playtower, Ladywell Road.
020 8690 7002

SE18
Greenwich Gym Club
Waterfront Leisure Centre, High Street
Woolwich. 020 8317 5000

SE19
Sports Workshop
Crystal Palace National Sports Centre.
020 8659 4561

SW10
Gymjams Ltd
4 Gilston Road. 020 7795 6086
And painting

SW14
Kids Works Ltd
020 8755 1583

SW18
Mayfield Gymnastics Club
020 8767 2094

SW19
TJ's Mini Gym
020 8640 2678

Wimbledon Leisure Centre
Latimer Road. 020 8542 1330
www.merton-leisure.co.uk

W2
Westminster Children's Sports Centre
Crompton Street. 020 7724 0038

W5
Ealing YMCA Health & Fitness Centre
25 St Mary's Road. 020 8799 4800
8mths-12yrs

W7
Crackerjack
99 Oaklands Road. 020 8840 3355
1yr+

W11
Jumping Jacks
The Tabernacle. 020 8960 8093

Tiny Tots Gym
Kensington Sports Centre, Walmer Road.
020 7727 9747

WC1
Bedford House Community Centre
35 Emerald Street. 020 7405 2370
Under 5s soft play area

Visit us at
www.babydirectory.com

hairdressers

Most hairdressers have a special chair attachment, and offer a cheap cut for kids *(if they can be bothered)*

SE10
Little Nippers
Plaza Arcade, 135 Vanbrugh Hill, Greenwich. 020 8293 4444

SW1
Harrods
Knightsbridge. 020 7730 1234
Certificate for first cut

W8
Trotters
127 Kensington High Street. 020 7937 9373

happiness

.... is a full night's sleep.
See page 192

health clubs with crèches

(see also exercise, leisure centres, personal trainers, swimming pools)

Listings are of private health clubs. Local sports centres often provide crèches to supplement their sports activities.

EC1
Holmes Place
97 Aldersgate Street. 020 7374 0091

N10
Dragons Health Club
Hillfield Road. 020 8444 8212

Manor Helath & Leisure Club
140 Fortis Green. 020 8883 0500

N16
Sunstone Health and Leisure Club
16 Northwold Road, Stoke Newington.
020 7923 1991
www.sunstonewomen.com

NW3
Lingfield Health Club
81 Belsize Park Gardens. 020 7722 8220

NW4
The Laboratory
Hall Lane. 020 8201 5500

SE15
Holmes Place at The Peckham Pulse
10 Melon Road. 020 7525 4990
Open to the public. Pool, play area, crèche, café

SE26
LA Fitness
291 Kirkdale. 020 8778 9818

SW6
Harbour Club
Watermeadow Lane. 020 7371 7700

SW7
DLL Health & Fitness Club
Point West, 116 Cromwell Road.
020 7259 2425

SW10
Holmes Place Chelsea
188a Fulham Road. 020 7352 9452

SW11
Cannon's Health Club
Sheepcote Lane. 020 7228 4400

SW15
Holmes Place Putney
Wellington House, 154-160 Upper Richmond Road. 020 8246 6676

SW19
Esporta Health and Fitness Club
21-33 Worple Road. 020 8545 1700

Holmes Place South Wimbledon
Battle Close, North Road. 020 8544 9111
www.holmesplace.co.uk

Tots Spot
Wimbledon Leisure Centre, Latimer Road.
020 8542 1330
www.merton-leisure.co.uk

W3
The Park Club
East Acton Lane. 020 8743 4321
www.hogarthgroup.co.uk

W4
Hogarth Health Club
1a Airedale Avenue. 020 8995 4600

Riverside Health Club
Duke's Meadows, Riverside Lane.
020 8994 9496

W5
Ealing YMCA Health & Fitness Centre
25 St Mary's Road. 020 8799 4800

Holmes Place Ealing
Level 5, Town Square, Ealing Broadway.
020 8579 9433

W6
Holmes Place Hammersmith
Galena House, Galena Road. 020 8741 8536

W11
Holmes Place Notting Hill
119-131 Lancaster Road. 020 7243 4141

WC1
Central London YMCA
112 Great Russell Street. 020 7343 1700
Crèche on Saturday

free advice and more

helplines

If you can't find what you're looking for here, try the index at the back of the book.

AIDS
Avert: National
Aids Helpline 0800 567123

Positively Women 020 7713 0222

allergy
British Allergy Foundation 020 8303 8583

anaphylaxis
Anaphylaxis Campaign 01252 542029
www.anaphylaxis.org.uk
Severe allergic reactions, e.g. to nuts

asthma
National
Asthma Campaign 020 7226 2260
www.asthma.org.uk

autism
National Autistic Society 020 7833 2299
www.nas.org.uk

bedwetting
Enuresis Resource & Information Centre
(ERIC) 0117 960 3060
www.eric.org.uk

bereavement
Bereaved Parents Network 029 2081 0800
c/o Care for the Family.

Child Bereavement Trust 01494 446648
www.childbereavement.org.uk

Child Death Helpline 0800 282986
Mon, Wed, Thu .

CRUSE Bereavement Care 020 8940 4818
info@crusecare.org.uk

Stillbirth and Neonatal Death Society
(SANDS) 020 7436 7940
support@uk-sands.org
www.uk-sands.org
Information and support for bereaved parents

birth
Birth Crisis Network 01865 300266

h

helplines (cont.)

Birth Defects Foundation 08700 707020
enquiries@birthdefects.co.uk

National Childbirth
Trust (NCT) 0870 4448707

blindness
LOOK (National Federation of
Families with Visually Impaired
Children) 0121 428 5038

RNIB 020 7391 2245

brain injury
British Institute for Brain Injured
Children (BIBIC) 01278 684060
www.bibic.org.uk

bullying
Anti-Bullying Campaign 020 7378 1446
For children bullied at school

Kidscape 020 7730 3300

caesarians
Caesarian Support Network .. 01624 661269
weekends 6-10pm

cerebral palsy
Cerebral Palsy Helpline
(SCOPE) 0808 8003333
www.scope.org.uk
Mon-Fri 9am-9pm. Weekends 2-6pm

children
Daycare Trust 020 7739 2866
info@daycaretrust.org.uk
National childcare campaign

ChildLine 0800 1111
www.childline.org.uk

Kid's Club Network 020 7512 2100
For parents, schools, playworkers

cleft lip
Cleft Lip and Palate
Association (CLAPA) 020 7431 0033
www.clapa.com

coeliac disease
Coeliac Society 01494 437278

cot death
Cot Death Helpline 0845 601 0234

Cot Death Society 01925 850086
www.cotdeathsociety.co.uk

Foundation for the Study
of Infant Deaths 020 7233 2090
fsid@sids.org.uk
www.sids.org.uk/fsid/
24-hr helpline

cruelty
NSPCC Child Protection
Helpline 0800 800 500

crying
Serene
(incorporating Cry-sis) 020 7404 5011
Helpline 8am-11pm

cystic fibrosis
Cystic Fibrosis Trust 020 8464 7211
www.cftrust.org.uk

deafness
National Deaf
Children's Society 020 7250 0123
General: 020 7490 8656

diabetes
Diabetes UK (ex-British Diabetes
Association) 020 7323 1531
www.diabetes.org.uk

disability
Contact-A-Family 020 7383 3555
www.cafamily.org.uk
Local parent support groups

Council for Disabled
Children 020 7843 6000
www.ncb.org.uk

Disability Alliance 020 7247 8763

divorce
Mediation in Divorce 020 8891 6860
admin@mediationindivorce.co.uk

down's syndrome
Down's Heart Group 01525 220379

h

Down's Syndrome
Association 020 8682 4001
info@downs-syndrome.org.uk
www.dsa.uk.com

dyslexia
British Dyslexia Association .. 0118 966 8271
See also learning difficulties

dyspraxia
Dyspraxia Foundation 01462 454986
For help with 'clumsy child syndrome'

eczema
National Eczema Society 020 7388 4097
www.eczema.org

education
Advisory Centre on
Education (ACE) 020 7354 8321
Advice 2-5pm

British Association for Early Childhood
Education 020 7539 5400

Children's Information
Service 0800 960296
www.childcarelink.gov.uk

epilepsy
British Epilepsy Association ..0113 2108800
www.epilepsy.org.uk

fatherhood
Families Need Fathers............ 020 7613 5060
www.fnf.org.uk
Advice for non-custodial parents

formula milk
Baby Milk Action 01223 464420
www.babymilkaction.org

fragile X
Fragile X Society 01424 813147

gifted children
National Association for
Gifted Children 01908 673 677

health
GP list 0800 665544

Health Information Service 0800 665544

NHS Direct...................................... 0845 4647
www.nhsdirect.nhs.uk
24-hr line

Women's Health 020 7251 6580
52-54 Featherstone Street, London EC1.
www.womenshealthlondon.org.uk
Gynaecological and sexual health.
Reference library and advice

herpes
Herpes Association 020 7609 9061

hyperactivity
ADISS Resource Centre 020 8906 9068
www.addiss.co.uk
Information, training, resources and
support nationally and locally. Put people
in touch with local support groups

Hyperactive Children's Support Group
01903 725182
10am-1pm

marriage
National Family Mediation .. 020 7383 5993
mediation@nfm.org.uk

Relate:
National Marriage Guidance 020 8367 7712
www.relate.org.uk

maternity services
Association for Improvements in the
Maternity Services(AIMS) 01753 652781

ME
Action for ME
Pregnancy Network 01749 670799

meningitis
National Meningitis Trust 0845 6000800
www.meningitis-trust.org.uk

miscarriage
Miscarriage Association 01924 200799
c/o Clayton Hospital, Wakefield.
www.miscarriageassociation.org.uk

motherhood
Full Time Mothers
PO Box 186, London SW3 5RF

multiple births
(see twins)

helplines (cont.)

parenthood
National NEWPIN 020 7358 5900
newpin@nationalnewpin.freeserve.co.uk

Parentline Plus 0808 8002222
www.parentline.plus.org.uk
For parents under stress

postnatal depression
Association for Postnatal
Illness 020 7386 0868
www.apni.org

pre-eclampsia
Action on Pre-Eclampsia
(APEX) helpline 020 8427 4217
Calls 10am-1pm

reading difficulties
National Advice Centre for Children with
Reading Difficulties 0845 604 0414

sexual abuse
SACCAA 020 8950 7855
sacca@hosfieldwatford.demon.co.uk

single parents
Gingerbread 020 7488 9300
www.gingerbread.org.uk

National Council
for One-Parent Families 08000 185 026
www.oneparentfamilies.org.uk

smoking
Quit... 020 7487 3000

stammering
British Stammering
Association 020 8983 1003
www.stammering.org

twins
Multiple Births Foundation .. 020 8383 3519
c/o Queen Charlotte's Hospital, London

Twins & Multiple Births 01732 868 8000
Helpline only 7-11pm evenings and
weekends. Weekdays: 0151 348 0020

violence
Women's Domestic
Violence Helpline 0161 839 8574

widowhood
The WAY Foundation 01222 711209

work
Parents at Work 020 7628 2128

LITTLE STARS
WE'RE HERE TO MAKE YOUR LIFE EASIER

Hire all your baby equipment from us today.

Tel: 020 8537 0980 or 020 8621 4378
www.littlestars.co.uk

Member of the Baby Equipment Hirers Association
It couldn't be easier

hiring equipment

(see also nearly new shops, party equipment)

Little Stars
020 8537 0980
www.littlestars.co.uk

Chelsea Baby Hire
020 8540 8830

Nappy Express
020 8361 4040

holiday play schemes

Local councils run grant-aided holiday
schemes. Independent schools, leisure
centres, swimming pools and private
companies offer their own programmes.

Art 4 Fun
Various locations
See advert under party entertainers

Camp Beaumont
Linton House, 164-180 Union Street,
London SE1. 0845 608 1234

NW3
Creative Wiz Kids
020 7794 6797
2-6 yrs, arts.
See advert under art

PGL Travel Ltd
Alton Court, 10 Yard Lane, Ross-on-Wye,
Herefordshire. 0500 749147
www.pgl.co.uk
6yrs+

home birth

(see also antenatal support & information)

National Childbirth Trust branches often have a home birth support group. If you get no joy from your GP, contact your local hospital's Director of Midwifery *(see hospitals)* or an independent midwife *(see midwives).*

home delivery services

(see also home birth)

Supermarkets such as Tesco and Sainsburys now deliver direct.

Organics Direct
020 7729 2828
www.organicsdirect.com

Food Ferry
020 7498 0827
www.foodferry.com

home education

Home Education Advisory Service
01707 371854
www.heas.co.uk

Student Support Centre
46 Church Avenue, Beckenham.
0800 917 8594

homoeopathy

(see also complementary health)

A plethora of 'national' organisations representing homoeopaths.

British Homoeopathic Association
15 Clerkenwell Close, London EC1.
020 7566 7800

College of Practical Homoeopathy
020 8346 7800
For a list of medically qualified homoeopaths, doctors, dentists and vets

Society of Homoeopaths
4a Artizan Road, Northampton.
01604 621400

United Kingdom Homoeopathic Medical Association
6 Livingstone Road, Gravesend, Kent.
01474 560336

■ *Local homoeopaths*
N1
Caroline Gaskin
020 7704 6900

SW/SE
Olga Lawrence Jones
020 7737 1294

SW16
Sunita Rastogi
020 8764 4562

W6
Dr Max Deacon
Medical Homoeopath. 020 7602 1006

Homoeopathic Children's Clinic
Brackenbury Natural Health Centre, 30 Brackenbury Road. 020 8741 9264

hospitals: dolls & teddies

The Doll and Teddy Hospital and Orphanage
Old Hill House, 53 Dover Street, Maidstone, Kent. 01622 727020

The Doll's Hospital
17 George Street, Hastings, East Sussex.
01424 444117

hospitals: NHS

In case of emergency call 999

Action for Sick Children
0800 074 4519
Help for parents with children in
hospital

E1
Royal London Hospital
Whitechapel. 020 7377 7000
Large general hospital with maternity,
obstetrics, paediatrics, accident and
emergency

E9
Homerton Hospital
Homerton Row. 020 8510 5555
Large teaching hospital, A&E, obstetrics, etc.

E11
Whipps Cross Hospital
Whipps Cross Road. 020 8539 5522
Maternity, accident & emergency

E13
Newham General Hospital
Glen Road, Plaistow. 020 7476 4000

EC1
St Bartholomew's Hospital
West Smithfield. 020 7377 7000
No accident & emergency. Minor injuries
clinic 8am-8pm. No obstetrics or maternity

Moorfields Eye Hospital
City Road. 020 7253 3411
24-hour eye accident & emergency.
Paediatric department

EN2
Chase Farm Hospital
The Ridgeway. 020 8366 6600
A & E, maternity, paediatrics

HA1
Northwick Park Hospital
Watford Road, Harrow. 020 8864 3232
Big teaching hospital

KT2
Kingston Hospital
Galsworthy Road, Kingston-upon-Thames.
020 8546 7711
General hospital with maternity, accident &
emergency, paediatrics

N18
North Middlesex Hospital
Sterling Way. 020 8887 2000
Large general hospital with maternity
wing, obstetrics departments. Accident &
emergency

N19
Whittington Hospital
Highgate Hill, Archway. 020 7272 3070
Large general hospital with maternity
wing, obstetrics departments. Accident &
emergency

NW1
Western Ophthalmic Hospital
Marylebone Road. 020 7886 6666
24-hour eye casualty

NW3
Royal Free Hospital
Pond Street, Hampstead. 020 7794 0500
Large general hospital with maternity wing
and obstetrics department. Paediatrics,
accident & emergency

NW10
Central Middlesex Hospital
Acton Lane, Park Royal. 020 8965 5733
Accident & emergency, maternity

SE1
Guy's Hospital
St Thomas Street. 020 7955 5000
Maternity, minor injury (also paediatric),
obstetrics

St Thomas' Hospital
Lambeth Palace Road. 020 7929 9292
Large general hospital with maternity,
obstetrics, paediatrics, accident &
emergency

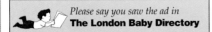

SE5
King's College Hospital
Denmark Hill, Camberwell. 020 7737 4000
Large teaching hospital hospital with
paediatrics, obstetrics, accident &
emergency

SE10
Greenwich District Hospital
Vanbrugh Hill. 020 8858 8141
Maternity, accident & emergency

SE13
Lewisham University Hospital
Lewisham High Street. 020 8333 3000
Accident & emergency, maternity,
paediatrics

SW10
Chelsea and Westminster Hospital
369 Fulham Road. 020 8746 8000
Large general hospital with maternity,
obstetrics, paediatrics, accident &
emergency (separate children's wing)

SW15
Queen Mary's University Hospital
Roehampton Lane. 020 8789 6611
No pregnant women or under fives! Minor
injuries unit

SW17
St George's Hospital
Blackshaw Road. 020 8672 1255
Large general hospital with maternity,
obstetrics, accident & emergency

SW6
Charing Cross Hospital
Fulham Palace Road. 020 8846 1234
Large general hospital. No obstetrics,
maternity or paediatrics. Accident &
emergency

TW7
West Middlesex Hospital
Twickenham Road, Isleworth. 020 8560
2121
Maternity, accident & emergency,
paediatrics

UB1
Ealing Hospital
Uxbridge Road, Southall. 020 8967 5000
Maternity, paediatrics, accident &
emergency

W12
Hammersmith Hospital
Du Cane Road. 020 8383 1000
Large general hospital with obstetrics,
paediatrics, accident & emergency.
Same site as Queen Charlotte's

**Queen Charlotte's and Chelsea
Hospital NHS Trust**
Du Cane Road. 020 8383 1000
www.hhnt.org
New building, opened December 2000 on
the same site as Hammersmith Hospital.
Maternity and obstetrics only. Two birthing
pools, 8 private beds. Supposedly state of
the art

W1
Middlesex Hospital
Mortimer Street. 020 7636 8333
Mostly at University College Hospital. See WC1

W2
St Mary's Hospital
Praed Street. 020 7886 6666
Large general hospital with maternity,
paediatrics, obstetrics, accident & emergency

WC1
**University College Hospital
(Obstetrics)**
Huntley Street. 020 7387 9300

University College Hospital
Grafton Way. 020 7387 9300
Large general hospital with maternity wing
in Huntley Street and obstetrics. Paediatrics,
accident & emergency

Hospital for Sick Children
Great Ormond Street. 020 7405 9200
No accident & emergency. Specialist
children's hospital

hospitals: private maternity

Many NHS hospitals offer private facilities or have a private wing

NW8
Hospital of St John & St Elizabeth
Grove End Road. 020 7286 5126
www.babydirectory.com/stjohn

SW17
Birth Centre
37 Coverton Road, Tooting. 020 7498 2322
www.birthcentre.com

W1
Portland Hospital
205-209 Great Portland Street. 020 7580 4400
www.theportlandhospital.com
Midwife-led delivery

W2
Lindo Wing
St Mary's Hospital, South Wharf Road.
020 7886 1465

hotels & holidays

(see also ski companies, travel companies specialising in children, travel with kids)

■ **General**

Maternal Bliss
020 7592 9557

Centerparcs Ltd
0990 200200

Disneyland
Marne-la-Vallee Cedex 4, France.
0870 50 30 303
20 miles east of Paris

The following offer special facilities for children and babies, ranging from crèches to child listening, playgrounds, pools, etc.

■ *Avon*
The Bath Spa Hotel
Sydney Road, Bath, Avon. 01225 444424

Woolley Grange Hotel
Woolley Green, Bradford on Avon.
01225 864705
www.luxuryfamilyhotel.com
Toys, nursery, swimming pool, cycles, etc

■ *Channel Isles*
Stocks Island Hotel
Manor Valley, Sark. 01481 832001
stocks@sark.net
Swimming pool, child-friendly island, family bedrooms

■ *Cornwall*
Bedruthan Steps Hotel
Mawgan Porth. 01637 860555

Carlyon Bay Hotel
Sea Road, St Austell. 01726 812304
Supervised playroom, indoor and outdoor swimming pools, play area

Fowey Hotel
Hanson Drive, Fowey. 01726 833866
Nursery, play area

Higher Lank Farm
St Breward, Bodmin. 01208 850716
Rural B&B for families

Polurrian
Mullion. 01326 240421

Sands Family Resort
Watergate Road, Porth. 01637 872864
Crèche, playground

St Martin's on the Isle
St Martin's, Isles of Scilly. 01720 422092
Pool, videos

Tredethy House Country Hotel
Helland Bridge, Bodmin. 01208 841262

Watergate Bay Hotel
Watergate Bay, Newquay. 01637 860543
hotel@watergate.com.uk

Wringford Down Hotel
Cawsand. 01752 822287

■ *Cumbria*
Stakis Lodore Swiss Hotel
Borrowdale, Keswick. 017687 77285

■ *Devon*
The Bulstone Hotel
Higher Bulstone, Branscombe, Sidmouth.
01297 680446
Play areas, high tea, children under 11yrs free

Gara Rock
East Portlemouth, Nr Salcombe,
South Devon. 01548 842342

Langstone Cliff Hotel
Dawlish. 01626 868000

Radfords County Hotel
Dawlish. 01626 863322

Saunton Sands Hotel
Nr Braunton, North Devon.
01271 890212
Nursery, pool

■ *Dorset*
Chine Hotel
25 Boscombe Spa Road, Bournemouth.
01202 396234

Fairfields Hotel
Studland Bay. 01929 450224

Knoll House
Studland Bay. 01929 450450
www.knollhouse.co.uk

THE
KNOLL HOUSE
STUDLAND BAY

ESTABLISHED 1931

A peaceful oasis and relaxing holiday for all ages
~
Secluded gardens with easy access to three miles of golden beach
Outdoor pool (level deck), golf, tennis, health spa
~
Connecting rooms for families and ground floor for the elderly
Children's restaurant, playroom and adventure playground
~
Daily full board terms: £93 - £118. Children much less, by age
Excellent low season offers
~
Open Easter - end October   Dogs also welcome

STUDLAND BAY
DORSET
BH19 3AH

ONLY 2 HOURS FROM HEATHROW

For Colour Brochure
TEL 01929 · 450450   FAX 01929 · 450423
Email: enquiries@knollhouse.co.uk
Website: www.knollhouse.co.uk

hotels & holidays (cont.)

Moonfleet Manor
Moonfleet, Weymouth. 01305 786 948
Indoor pool, creche, playground

Sandbanks Hotel
15 Banks Road, Sandbanks, Poole.
01202 707377
Playroom, babysitting

■ *Gloucestershire*
Calcot Manor
Tetbury, Gloucestershire. 01666 890391

■ *Hampshire*
Watersplash Hotel
The Rise, Brockenhurst. 01590 622344
Outdoor pool

■ *Hertfordshire*
Marriott Hanbury Manor
Nr Sandridge, Ware. 01920 487722
Crèche, pool

■ *Inverness*
Polmaily House Hotel
Drumnadrochit, Loch Ness. 01456 450343
Babysitting, children's activities

■ *Isle of Wight*
The Clarendon Hotel - The Wight Mouse Inn
Chale. 01983 730431

■ *London*
Charoscuro at Townhouse
24 Coptic Street, WC1. 020 7636 2731

Days Inn Hotel
54 Kennington Road, Waterloo,
London SE1. 020 7922 1331

London County Hall Travel Inn Capital
Belvedere Road, London SE1. 020 7902 1600

myhotel
11-13 Bayley Street, Bedford Square,
London WC1. 020 7636 0076

■ *Norfolk*
Heath Farm House B & B
Homersfield, Harleston. 01986 788417

■ *Perthshire*
Gleneagles Hotel
Auchterarder. 01764 662231
Playground, creche

■ *Wiltshire*
Old Bell
Abbey Row, Malmesbury. 01666 822344

■ *Worcestershire*
Evesham Hotel
Coopers Lane, Off Waterside, Evesham.
01386 765566

hypnotherapy

British Hypnotherapy Association
67 Upper Berkeley Street, London W1.
020 7723 4443

National Hypnotherapy Enquiries
01282 699378

E7
Pauline Grant
020 8555 3698

N10
Debra Sequoia
169 Avenue Mews, Muswell Hill.
020 8365 3545
Self-hypnosis, hypnotherapy

W6
Mellennium Clinic
Richford Gate Primary Care Centre,
Richford Street. 020 8846 7539
www.mellenniumclinic.co.uk

Hypnonatal Program
hypnonatal@ukonline.co.uk

h

ice rinks

E10
Lea Valley Ice Centre
Lea Bridge Road. 020 8533 3154

EC2
Broadgate Ice
Broadgate Circle. 020 7505 4068

N7
Sobell Leisure Centre
Hornsey Road. 020 7609 2166

N22
Alexandra Palace Ice Rinks
Alexandra Palace Way, Wood Green.
020 8365 2121
3yrs+

SW16
Streatham Ice Arena
386 Streatham High Road. 020 8769 7771

W2
Leisurebox
17 Queensway. 020 7229 0172

indoor adventure playcentres

Local leisure centres may also have indoor
play areas.

E5
Kids Mania
28 Powell Road, Clapton. 020 8533 5556

E11
Soft Play Activity Sessions
Cathall Leisure Centre, Cathall Road.
020 8539 8343

N5
The Play House
The Old Gymnasium, Highbury Grove
School, Highbury New Park. 020 7704 9424

N7
Pirates Playhouse
Sobell Leisure Centre, Hornsey Road.
020 7609 2166

N9
Tropical Adventure Trail
Lea Valley Leisure Centre, Picketts Lock
Lane, Edmonton. 020 8345 6666

Fun House
Edmonton Leisure Centre, Plevna Road.
020 8807 0712

N12
Clown Town
Coppetts Centre, Colney Hatch Lane,
Finchley. 020 8361 6600

N15
Toddler Bounce
Tottenham Green Leisure Centre,
Phillip Lane. 020 8489 5322

N19
**Highgate Newtown Community
Centre Skate and Bounce**
25 Bertram Street. 020 7272 7201
hncc@camvolsec12.demon.co.uk

N22
Playstation
2a Brabant Road, Wood Green.
020 8889 0001

NW3
Under 5s Gym
Swiss Cottage Sports Centre,
Winchester Road. 020 7413 6490

NW6
**Sidings Community Centre Under 5s
Soft Room**
150 Brassey Road. 020 7625 6260
Inflatable castle Tues, Thurs

SE5
Camberwell Leisure Centre
Artichoke Place, Camberwell Church Street.
020 7703 3024

SE10
Toddlers' World
Arches Leisure Centre, 80 Trafalgar Road.
020 8317 5000

SE13
Kid's Corner
232 Hither Green Lane. 020 8852 3322

SE16
Discovery Planet
Surrey Quays Shopping Centre,
Redriff Road, Surrey Quays. 020 7237 2388

indoor adventure playcentres (cont.)

SE18
Rascals
Waterfront Leisure Centre, High Street,
Woolwich. 020 8317 5000

SE19
Spike's Madhouse
Crystal Palace National Sports Centre.
020 8778 9876

SE26
House of Fun
The Bridge Leisure Centre,
Kangley Bridge Road, Sydenham.
020 8778 7158

SW15
Buttercups
Roehampton Parish Hall, Alton Road.
0961 100425

SW17
Kidzone
Balham Leisure Centre, Elmfield Road.
020 8772 9577

SW19
Tiger's Eye
42 Station Road, Merton Abbey Mills.
020 8543 1655

TW8
Little Tikes
Brentford Fountain Leisure Centre,
Chiswick High Road. 020 8994 9596

Snakes and Ladders
Syon Park, Brentford. 020 8847 0946

TW9
Lollipop Club
Old Deer Park, 187 Kew Road.
020 8332 7436

W10
Bramley's Big Adventure
136 Bramley Road. 020 8960 1515

W11
Bumper's Backyard
Kensington Sports Centre, Walmer Road.
020 7727 9747

infertility

CHILD - National Infertility Support Network
01424 732361

Human Fertilisation and Embryology Authority
Paxton House, 30 Artillery Lane, E1.
020 7377 5077

National Fertility Association
0121 344 4414

www.zitawest.com
08701 668899
See advert under nutrition

Portland Hospital
205-209 Great Portland Street, W1.
020 7580 4400
www.theportlandhospital.com
See advert under hospitals, private maternity

internet

(see also web sites)

Try your local library – the wealthier ones may offer terminals, with easy buggy access. Don't forget to look us up on **www.babydirectory.com.**

italian

(see also french clubs & classes)

Italian Au Pairs
020 8946 5728

EC1
Filef
96-98 Central Street. 020 7608 0125

SW
Italian Club
020 8287 7420
$3^1/_2$yrs+

SW6
Il Club Italiano
020 8748 6418

SW9
Italian Day Nursery
174 Clapham Road. 020 7735 3058
3-5yrs

japanese

W1
Japan Centre
212 Piccadilly. 020 7439 8035

W3
Japanese Recycle Shop
18 Queens Drive. 020 8991 0334

Japanese School
87 Creffield Road. 020 8993 7145
Co-ed 8-14yrs

London Bunka Yochien
Holy Family Church, Vale Lane.
020 8992 9822
Nursery 2-5yrs

learning difficulties

(see also helplines)

**British Institute for Learning
Disabilities**
01562 850251
www.bild.org.uk

NW3
Willoughby Hall Dyslexia Centre
1 Willoughby Road. 020 7794 3538
6-12yrs

SW11
David Mulhall Centre
31 Webbs Road. 020 7223 4321

SW18
**Hornsby International Dyslexia
Centre**
261 Trinity Road. 020 8874 1844
3yrs+

left-handedness

Anything Lefthanded
57 Brewer Street, London W1. 020 7437 3910
Mail order: 020 8770 3722

legal advice

Your local Citizen's Advice Bureau is a
good starting point. The local library
reference department may also be able to
help.

Children's Legal Centre
01206 873 820

Education Law Association
01303 211570
Contact for a list of solicitors in your area

www.freelawyer.co.uk

Charles Russell
8-10 New Fetter Lane, EC4. 020 7203 5000
www.charlesrussell.co.uk

Nucleus Legal Advice Centre
298 Old Brompton Road, SW5.
020 7373 4005
nucleus@dial.pipex.com
Drop-in

North Kensington Law Centre
74 Golborne Road, W10. 020 8969 7473
Free legal advice on domestic violence,
juvenile crime, housing, education, etc

More information on-line

leisure centres

(see also health clubs with crèches, swimming pools)

Leisure centres with swimming facilities are listed under swimming pools

E5
King's Hall Leisure Centre
39 Lower Clapton Road. 020 8985 2158

N7
Sobell Leisure Centre
Hornsey Road. 020 7609 2166

NW2
Hendon Youth Sports Centre
Marble Drive. 020 8455 0818

NW6
Charteris Sports Centre
24 Charteris Road. 020 7625 6451

SW19
Wimbledon Leisure Centre
Latimer Road. 020 8542 1330
www.merton-leisure.co.uk

W3
Bromyard Leisure Centre
36 Bromyard Avenue. 020 8749 2282

Reynolds Sports Centre
Gunnersbury Lane. 020 8993 9092
5yrs+

Twyford Sports Centre
Twyford Crescent. 020 8993 9095
3yrs+

W4
Chiswick Sports Hall
Chiswick Community School, Burlington Hall. 020 8995 4067
Gym, trampolining, football, etc

W7
Elthorne Sports Centre
Westlea Road. 020 8579 3226
Trampolining 4yrs+

Visit us at
www.babydirectory.com

libraries

(see also toy libraries)

You and your children can join local libraries free of charge on proof of residence and borrow books, videos and cassettes. A fantastic resource, libraries are also a good source of local information. Days and times refer to storytime sessions. Some libraries run additional activity classes in the school holidays.

E4
North Chingford Library
The Green, Station Road. 020 8529 2993

E5
Clapton Library
Northwold Road. 020 8356 2570

E8
CLR James Library
24-30 Dalston Lane. 020 8356 2572

E9
Homerton Library
Homerton High Street. 020 8356 2572

EC1
Finsbury Library
245 St John Street. 020 7689 7960

N1
Islington Central Library
Fieldway Crescent.
Crèche Mon am

Lewis Carroll Children's Library
180 Copenhagen Street. 020 7619 7936
Under 5s Fri 9.3am. Under 3s Thurs am

Mildmay Park Library
21-23 Mildmay Park

Shoreditch Library
80 Hoxton Street. 020 8356 4350

South Library
115/117 Essex Road. 020 7619 7860

West Library
2 Bridgeman Road. 020 7619 7920
Closed Mons

N4
Arthur Simpson Library
Hanley Road

N6
Highgate Library
Shepherd's Hill. 020 8348 3443
Tues 2pm

N8
Hornsey Library
Haringey Park. 020 8489 1427

N9
Edmonton Green Library
South Mall, Edmonton Green

N10
Muswell Hill Library
Queens Avenue. 020 8883 6734
Mon 2.45pm, Thurs 11am

N11
Bowes Road Library
Bowes Road. 020 8368 2085

N13
Palmers Green Library
Broomfield Lane. 020 8886 3728

N14
Southgate Circus Library
High Street. 020 8882 8849

N15
Marcus Garvey Library
Tottenham Green Centre, 1 Philip Lane.
020 8489 5309

St Ann's Library
Cissbury Road, Tottenham. 020 8800 4390
Toy library Mon, Fri, Sat

West Green Libraries
West Green Primary School, Terrant Road

N16
Stamford Hill Library
Portland Avenue. 020 8356 2573

Stoke Newington Library
184 Stoke Newington Church Street.
020 8356 5231
Sat 11am

N17
Coombes Croft Library
Tottenham High Road. 020 8808 0022

N19
Archway Library
Hamlyn House, Highgate Hill

Highgate Library
Chester Road. 020 7860 5752
Tues 2-3.30pm

N21
Ridge Avenue Library
Ridge Avenue. 020 8360 9662

Winchmore Hill Library
Green Lanes. 020 8360 8344

N22
Alexandra Park Library
Alexandra Park Road. 020 8883 8553

Wood Green Central Library
High Road. 020 8888 1292

NW1
Camden Town Library
Crowndale Centre, 218 Eversholt Street.
020 7619 7974
Tues 2.30-4pm

Chalk Farm Library
Sharpleshall Street. 020 7619 6526
Fri 10.30am-12pm

Marylebone Library
109-117 Marylebone Road. 020 7641 1041
Tues 10am

Queen's Crescent Library
Queen's Crescent. 020 7413 6243

Regent's Park Library
Compton Close, off Robert Street.
020 7974 1530
Thurs 11am

NW3
Belsize Branch Library
Antrim Road. 020 7413 6518
Tues 10.30-11.45am

Heath Library
Keats Grove. 020 7619 6520
Mon 10.30am during holidays

Swiss Cottage Library
88 Avenue Road. 020 7619 6522
Mon & Wed am, mother & toddler group

NW5
Kentish Town Library
262-6 Kentish Town Road. 020 7619 6523
Thurs 2-3.30pm

NW6
Kilburn Library
Cotleigh Road. 020 7619 1965
Thurs 11am

West Hampstead Library
Dennington Park Road. 020 7619 6610
Thurs 10.30am-12pm

NW8
Church Street Library
Church Street. 020 7641 5479
Weds 10am

libraries (cont.)

St John's Wood Library
20 Circus Road. 020 7641 5087
Thurs 10am

SE1
East Street Library
168-170 Old Kent Road. 020 7703 0395
Thurs 10.30am

John Harvard Library
211 Borough High Street. 020 7407 0807
Tues 10.30am

SE3
Blackheath Village Library
3-4 Blackheath Grove. 020 8852 5309
Last Thurs of the month, 11-11.30am

SE5
Camberwell Library
17-21 Camberwell Church Street.
020 7703 3763
Mon 10.30am-12.00pm, playgroup

Minet
25 Knatchbull Road. 020 7926 6073
Homework club, CD Roms, etc. Mon 1-3pm

SE11
Durning Library
167 Kennington Lane. 020 7926 8682
Thurs 11am

SE13
Lewisham Library
199-201 Lewisham High Street.
020 8297 9677
Tues 10am

SE15
Nunhead Library
Gordon Road. 020 7639 0264
Mon 10am

SE16
Blue Anchor Library
Market Place. 020 7231 0475
Homework club, classes, etc

Rotherhithe Library
Albion Street. 020 7237 2010

SE19
Upper Norwood Library
39 Westow Hill, Crystal Palace.
020 8670 2551
Tues sessions

SE21
Kingwood Library
Seeley Drive, Dulwich. 020 8670 4803
Homework club, story sessions, etc

SE22
Dulwich Library
368 Lordship Lane. 020 8693 5171
Thurs 10.30am

Grove Vale Library
25-27 Grove Vale, East Dulwich.
020 8693 5734
Tues 10.30am

SE23
Forest Hill Library
Dartmouth Road. 020 8699 2065
Tues under 5s.
First Thurs each month 6-11yr olds

SE26
Sydenham Library
Sydenham Road. 020 8778 7563
Thurs sessions

SW1
Churchill Gardens Children's Library
Ranelagh Grove. 020 7931 7978

Pimlico Library
Rampayne Street. 020 7641 2983
Tues 10am

Victoria Library
160 Buckingham Palace Road.
020 7641 4289
Weds 10am-12pm

SW3
Chelsea Library
Old Town Hall, Kings Road. 020 7352 6056
Fri 11.30am

SW4
Clapham Library
The Old Town, 1 Clapham Common
Northside. 020 7926 0717

Clapham Park Library
Poinders Road.
Mon 2pm

SW5
Brompton Library
210 Old Brompton Road. 020 7373 3111
Wed 10-12pm

SW6
Fulham Library
598 Fulham Road. 020 8576 5255
Tues 2.15pm

Sands End Library Community Centre
59-61 Broughton Road. 020 8576 5257

SW8
Tate South Lambeth Library
180 South Lambeth Road. 020 7926 0705
Wed

SW11
Battersea Library
Lavender Hill. 020 8871 7466
Closed Thurs

Battersea Park Library
309 Battersea Park Road. 020 8871 7468
Fri 2.30pm

Northcote Library
Northcote Road. 020 8871 7469
Tues 10.30-12.30

York Library
Lavender Road. 020 8871 7471
Thurs 2-2.30pm

SW12
Balham Library
Ramsden Road. 020 8871 7195

SW13
Castelnau Library
75 Castelnau, Barnes. 020 8748 3837
Wed 2.30pm

SW14
East Sheen Library
Sheen Lane, East Sheen. 020 8876 8801
Wed 2.30pm

SW15
Putney Library
Disraeli Road. 020 8871 7090
Mon-Tues 2.30pm

Roehampton Library
Danebury Avenue

SW18
Alvering Library
Allfarthing Lane, Wandsworth.
020 8871 6398
Mon 2.45pm (subject to staff availability)

Earlsfield Library
Magdalen Road. 020 8871 6389

Westhill Library
West Hill. 020 8871 6386
Tues 2.30pm

SW19
Donald Hope Library
Cavendish House,
Colliers Wood High Street. 020 8542 1975
Thurs 2.15pm

Southfields Library
Wimbledon Park Road. 020 8871 6388
Tues 10.30, Wed 2pm

Wimbledon Library
Wimbledon Hill Road. 020 8946 7432
Tues 2.15pm, Fri 11.15am

SW20
Raynes Park Library
Approach Road. 020 8543 6132
Tues 2.30pm

W1
Mayfair Library
25 South Audley Street. 020 7641 4903
Weds 10am

St James's Library
62 Victoria Street. 020 7641 2989

W2
Notting Hill Gate Library
1 Pembridge Square. 020 7229 8574
Fri 10.30am

Paddington Library
Porchester Road. 020 7641 4472
Weds 10am

W3
Acton Library
High Street. 020 8752 0999
Tues 2pm

W4
Chiswick Library
Duke's Avenue. 020 8994 1008
Mons 2.30pm

W5
Central Library
103 The Broadway Centre. 020 8567 3670

Northfields Library
Northfields Avenue. 020 8567 5700
Fri 11am

Pitshanger Library
143-145 Pitshanger Lane. 020 8997 0230

W6
Hammersmith Children's Library
Shepherds Bush Road. 020 8576 5052
First Sat of each month 10.15am

W7
Hanwell Library
Cherington Road. 020 8567 5041

libraries (cont.)

W8
Kensington Central Library
Phillimore Walk, Hornton Street.
020 7937 2542
Tues 10am

W9
Maida Vale Library
Sutherland Avenue. 020 7641 3659
Mon 10am-12pm

W10
Kensal Library
20 Golborne Road. 020 8969 7736

Queens Park Library
666 Harrow Road. 020 7641 4575
Fri 10am

W11
North Kensington Library
108 Ladbroke Grove. 020 7727 6583
Mon 10.30am

W12
Askew Road Library
87-91 Askew Road. 020 8576 5064
First Sat of month, 11am.

Shepherds Bush Children's Library
7 Uxbridge Road. 020 8576 5062
Tues 10.30am

W13
West Ealing Library
Melbourne Avenue. 020 8567 2812
Tues 10.30am, 2.30pm

W14
Baron's Court Library
North End Crescent, North End Road.
020 8576 5258

WC1
Holborn Library
32-38 Theobald Road. 020 7619 6358
Fri 10am-12pm

St Pancras Library
Town Hall Extension, Argyle Street.
020 7619 5833

WC2
Charing Cross Library
4 Charing Cross Road. 020 7641 4628

Westminster Reference Library
35 St Martin's Street. 020 7641 4636

lice

Head Lice Repellent
01597 823964
www.lice.co.uk

Verde
www.verde.co.uk

Olga Lawrence Jones
020 7737 1294
Homoeopathic treatments

life assurance

Rebroke Limited
1st Floor, Victoria Buildings, Middlewich,
Cheshire.
08000 852514
www.rebroke.com

More on-line help available

Baby★baby®
soft and snug for small people

Swedish styled bedding, pyjamas, blankets, slippers, fleece tops and lots more. Everything made in the softest materials.
For Mail-order or Stockists please call

020 8876 3153
www.babybabycompany.com

fig.
Children's Traditional Nightwear
01394 389 069
call for brochure

THE NURSERY COMPANY
'night, night, sleep tight'
a classic range of baby sleeping bags, bedlinen and nightwear in beautiful quality, natural fabrics for MAIL ORDER or suppliers please call
020 8878 5167
www.nurserycompany.co.uk

The BABY Directory SHOP
www.babydirectory.com

magazines

Families Magazine

News-filled magazines with useful local information for parents with young children.
Monthly free in selected outlets or by subscription, £15.50 for ten issues.

www.familiesmagazine.co.uk
Families South East
PO Box 11591, Sydenham, SE26 6WB.
020 8699 7240
familiesSE@aol.com

Families South West
PO Box 4302, London SW16 1ZS.
020 8696 9680
editor@familiesmagazine.co.uk

Families North West
PO Box 22358, Families North West, W13 8GQ.
020 8810 5388
FamiliesNorWest@aol.com

Families West
PO Box 10820, London W4 5GX.
020 8810 7008

Kids Out
Universal House,
251 Tottenham Court Road. W1. 020 7813 6018
Monthly family events magazine.
Available in newsagents.

Parents' Guide
Studio 234, Bon Marche Centre,
241-251 Ferndale Road,SW9.
020 7733 4955
lpg@talk21.com

SW/NW Parents' Directory
Bi-annual free booklet. 01243 527 605

Please say you saw the ad in
The London Baby Directory

m

Look out for your local quality FREE magazine

London area:
Families South West
Families South East
Families North
Families North West
Families West
Families Upon Thames
Families East

New areas:
(consult web)

Families Edinburgh

or subscribe to get the edition for your area!

Available free in selected shops, after school clubs and nurseries – to be <u>sure</u> of your copy, send £15.50 payable to: Families, PO Box 4302, SW16 1ZS saying which edition you need.

Families newsletters are above all: local info, features, events and local services.
Written by mothers who have lived in the area for years, they are practical and informative.
020 8696 9680 or editor@FamiliesMagazine.co.uk for information or to ask about franchise opportunities.

find local info on www.FamiliesMagazine.co.uk

The Parents'Guide

The original family magazine - essential information for parents and carers of children aged up to 14

◆In depth articles on health, education, travel, days out and activities. All you need to know to make the right decisions for your family.

◆Nationwide 'what's on' listings.

◆Extensive book, audio tape and software reviews.

Whatever help you need, whether it's information on asthma, a location for a great family holiday or a fantastic party entertainer, you'll find it in The Parents' Guide.

Published six times a year at £2.95. Available at good newsagents, supermarkets and bookshops as well as at selected children's clothes shops and by subscription. For stockist and subscription information, call 020 7733 4955.

mail order

accessories

Bagadele
01263 710200
Changing bags

Bebe Amour
01494 819914
www.bebeamour.co.uk

Blankets by Lisa
00 1 915 684 5353
www.blanketsbylisa.com
Personalised blankets

Children's TV Merchandising Ltd
020 8863 1112

Favourite Things
01932 355603

Full Moon Futons
0118 926 5648
Cotton cot mattresses

Hoppa Board Ltd
020 8809 4097
www.hoppaboard.co.uk

Izzi Designs Ltd
01273 479191
Changing mats

Kapoochi UK Ltd
0800 1383400
Changing mats

www.pottypaper.com
Potty training starter kit

www.room-in-a-box.co.uk
020 8404 6666

Synder Hills Handmade Hats
020 8761 7346

Tummy Tub
01256 851029

mail order (cont.)

aromatherapy
(see main section)

baby goods

Great Little Trading Company
08702 41 40 81
cat@gltc.co.uk
www.gltc.co.uk
See advert on page 77

The Green People Company Ltd
01444 401444

Little Green Earthlets Ltd
01825 873301
www.earthlets.co.uk

Mothercare Direct
01923 240365

Nippers
0800 594 3055

The Nursery Emporium plc
01380 859171
www.nursery-emporium.com

Perfectly Happy People Ltd (PHP)
0870 607 0545
www.phpbaby.com

Sleepy Bunnies
01865 300310
sleepybunn@aol.com
www.sleepybunnies.com

Snuggle Naps
0115 910 7220

Spirit of Nature Ltd
01582 847370

Tesco
0345 024024

Urchin Mail Order Ltd
01672 871515
www.urchin.co.uk

books

Barefoot Books
020 7704 6492
www.barefoot-books.com

Ragged Bears Learning Journey
01963 251018
www.raggedbears.co.uk

carriers

Better Baby Sling
01923 444442
www.betterbabysling.co.uk

Hippychick Ltd
01278 671461
www.hippychickltd.co.uk

Huggababy Natural Baby Products
01874 711629
www.huggababy.co.uk

Wilkinet
0800 138 3400
www.wilkinet.co.uk

clothing

Ant Eater Togs
020 8885 4711

Baby Bunting
01793 852306

www.babybabycompany.com
020 8876 3153
See advert under linens

www.beamingbaby.com
0800 0345 672
See advert under nappies

Children's Warehouse
020 8752 1166
www.childrens-warehouse.com

ClothWORKS
020 8299 1619

Cotton Moon Ltd
020 8305 0012
www.cottonmoon.com

Cyrillus
020 7734 6660
www.cyrillus.com

Debbie Bliss
020 7833 8255
www.debbiebliss.freeserve.co.uk

Dimples Baby Wear
020 7352 9240
dimples@foleymarsh.com

Emma Henley of Bath
01225 466835

mail order (cont.)

Gale Classic Clothes
01249 712241

Hansel and Gretel
01333 360219
www.hansel-and-gretel.co.uk

JoJo Maman Bebe
020 7924 6844
www.jojomamanbebe.co.uk
See advert on page 86

www.Jokids.com

Katie Mawson's Clothes for Children
020 7326 1880

Kids Gear
020 8977 1071
info@kids-gear.co.uk

Kids' Stuff
08702 41 40 61
www.kids-stuff.co.uk
See advert on page 77

www.kidzklobber.com

Kind Hearts Clothing
01225 700444
kindhearts_clothing@yahoo.com

Marks & Spencer Direct
0345 091011

Mini Boden
020 8453 1535
www.boden.co.uk

Mitty James
020 8693 5018
info@mittyjames.demon.co.uk

Outdoor Kids
01789 414791
www.outdoorkids.co.uk

www.overthemoon-babywear.co.uk
01625 502842

Patricia Smith
01736 793188

Rachel Riley
020 7259 5969
www.rachelriley.com

Raindrops
01730 810031
www.raindrops.co.uk

Ranch Mail
020 7372 8008

RJ's
01455 844477
www.rjcs.co.uk

Schmidt Natural Clothing
01342 822169

Silkstory
0800 150874
www.silkstory.com

Start Smart
01527 821766
www.startsmart.co.uk

Strawberry Kids
www.strawberrykids.com

Susu Mama Worldwear
020 7436 6768
www.susumama.co.uk

www.teeny-tots.com
0115 9663407

Tots & Teens
01765 604003

Trotters
0990 331 1888
www.trotters.co.uk

Vertbaudet
0500 012345
www.vertbaudet.co.uk.

fancy dress
(see main section)

flower essences

Little Miracles
020 7431 6153
www.littlemiracles.co.uk
Flower remedies
See advert under complementary therapy

gifts
(see main section)

home delivery
(see main section)

linens
(see main section)

maternity wear
(see main section)

nursery furniture
(see also main section)

Alice Hart & Company
020 8663 1248
www.alicehart.co.uk

Bettersleep Baby Bed
01869 811099
www.birthandbeyond.co.uk

Billie Bond Designs
01245 360164
www.billiebond.co.uk

Dragons of Walton Street
020 7589 3795
Hand-painted children's furniture
See advert on page 151

The Funbed Company
01753 642642
Themed beds for 2yrs+

Oreka Kids
020 8884 3435
www.oreka.com

Ragazzi Nursery Furniture
01993 774601
www.ragazzi.com

Shelf Life
01283 711282
Hand-crafted shelves

To the Manor Barn
01672 811713
www.tothemanorbarn.co.uk

Tots to Teens Furniture
01438 815355
See advert on page 150

Twinkle Twinkle
0118 934 2120

Willey Winkle
01432 268018
www.willeywinkle.co.uk
Organic mattresses
See advert on page 150

organic
(see main section)

shoes
Daisy Roots
01604 505616
www.daisy-roots.com

goo-goo gear
07002 466 466
www.goo-goo.com

Inch Blue
01222 865863

sleeping bags
(see main section)

toys
Acorn Toy Company
020 7371 8728
www.acorntoys.co.uk

mail order (cont.)

American Toys
01952 281905
www.americantoys.co.uk

www.beamingbaby.com
0800 0345 672
Natural & Organic Products for
Mother & Baby
See advert under nappies

Children's Cottage Company
01363 772061
www.play-houses.com

Dawson & Son
01799 526611
www.dawson-and-son.com

Formative Fun
01297 489880

Galt Premier Education
0161 637 2000

Harrison International
020 8398 6623

Hill Toy Company
0870 607 1248

Insect Lore Europe
01908 563338
www.insectlore.com
Butterfly kits and other equipment

Kula
020 8364 4641
www.kula.co.uk

Letterbox
0870 600 7878

Manhattan Toy
08700 129090
www.mailorderexpress.co.uk

Mulberry Bush Ltd
01403 785885
www.mulberry-bush.com

Play Horse Designs
01438 715819

The Playstore
www.playstore.com

Queenswood Puzzles
01953 883330

Spottiswoode Trading
01903 733123

Stuart Lennie
01453 750791

Toy Chest
01923 857553
www.toychest.co.uk

TP Activity Toys
www.tp-online.co.uk
Climbing frames

Treasure Chest
01829 770787

tridias
0870 240 2104
www.tridias.com

videos

Formative Years
01342 826555
www.formativeyears.co.uk

massage for baby & mother

Various venues
Millpond
020 8444 0040

Aromaware
020 8341 2714
See advert under aromatherapy

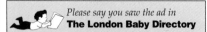

Crêchendo Training
1 Grange Mills, Weir Road. 020 8772 8160
training@crechendo.com
www.crechendo.com
See advert under first aid

E8
Baby Massage Group
Holistic Health, 64 Broadway Market.
020 7275 8434
holistic.health@virgin.net

N1
Fiona Curran
29 Old Royal Free Square, Liverpool Road,
Islington. 020 7354 9303
Midwife trained. Not pregnant women

N2
Na'ama Rogers
07930 312 950
Pregnant women

N7
Fit Start
Sobell Leisure Centre, Hornsey Road.
020 8374 7680
See advert under exercise

N10
Amber White
Muswell Healing Arts, 169 Avenue Mews.
020 8365 3545

N21
Ruth Sands
020 8360 5672

NW1
Fit Start
Mornington Sports Centre. 020 8374 7680
See advert under exercise

NW3
Baby Massage
Erskine Road, Primrose Hill. 020 7483 3344
www.triyoga.com

NW3/NW6
Alison Lidstone
07769 971331

massage for baby & mother (cont.)

NW7
Margarita Grant
020 8445 3669

SE12
Lu McLaren
020 8857 1668

SW2
Brigette Hass
79 Brixton Hill. 020 8671 5390
Yogic massage, healing, relaxation,
before and during pregnancy, reduce
stress, prepare for birth

SW13/SW14/SW15
From Bumps to Babies
020 8546 0532

SW17/18/19/20
Jan Littlemore
020 8287 5703
Infant massage instructor

W1
Brigette Hass
c/o Nature Works, 16 Balderton Street.
020 8671 5390
Yogic massage, healing, relaxation,
before and during pregnancy, reduce
stress, prepare for birth

W4
Louise Smith
07957 202291
Shiatsu too

W8
The Life Centre
15 Edge Street. 020 7221 4602
See advert under complementary medicine

W13
Ella van Meelis
020 8537 9258
ellaVanMeelis@aol.com

W14
Milson Road Health Centre
1-13 Milson Road. 020 8846 6262
Women and babies

maternity nannies

(see also doulas, midwives, nanny agencies)

Nannies Incorporated
Room 317 The Linen Hall,
162-168 Regent Street, W1. 020 7437 8989

Elite Nannies
22 Rowena Crescent, SW11. 020 7801 0061
See advert under nannies

Tinies Childcare
0800 783 6070
www.tinieschildcare.co.uk

Top Notch Nannies
49 Harrington Gardens, SW7.
020 7259 2626
See advert under nannies

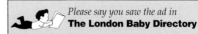

Please say you saw the ad in
The London Baby Directory

NANNIES INCORPORATED

Specialists in Maternity Care

Nannies Incorporated was established in 1989. We have 12 years experience in providing maternity nurses and nannies in London, country and overseas.

Please ask for a copy of our complimentary childcare guide for parents and consult our website.

MATERNITY NURSES

Our maternity nurses are trained or experienced nurses/nannies, registered nurses, midwives or health visitors who specialise in the care of the newborn, including multiple births.

All our maternity nurses are interviewed personally and have their references verified.

A maternity nurse will advise you in all aspects of feeding (breast/bottle), care and hygiene and assist you in establishing a suitable routine. They are on call 24 hours a day, 6 days a week. Advance bookings advisable.

LIVE IN AND DAILY NANNIES

Nannies Incorporated believe that creating a loving and stimulating environment for your children can only be achieved by adopting a professional interview and selection procedure. All our nannies are interviewed personally and have their references verified. We always seek to provide for the different needs and individual circumstances of our families.

Our nannies will either hold the NNEB, BTEC or similar qualification, will be privately trained or will have considerable experience.

317 THE LINEN HALL 162-168 REGENT STREET, LONDON W1R 5TD
TEL: 020 7437 8989 FAX: 020 7437 8889 E-MAIL: NanniesInc@aol.com
WEBSITE: http://www.nanniesinc.com

m

Have the best!

Maternity & Nursing Bra

For Brochure call: Body Comfort Ltd
Tel/Fax: 020 8459 2910
Email: nursing.bras@virgin.net
www.maternitybras.co.uk

Complete maternity collection

Adorable baby & kids' clothes

Nursery products & toys

Call for a free 76 page catalogue

0870 241 0451

or write to: JoJo Maman Bébé, 72 Bennerley Road, London SW11 6DS quoting TBD11

www.JoJoMamanBebe.co.uk
Order via our website and receive **FREE postage & packing** on orders over £60

www.babydirectory.com

maternity wear: mail order

Blooming Marvellous
020 8391 4822
www.bloomingmarvellous.co.uk

Bravado Maternity/Nursing Bra
020 8459 2910
nursing.bras@virgin.net

Budget Bumps
01427 810071
www.budget-bumps.co.uk

Bumpstart
020 8879 3467
www.bumpstart.co.uk

Business Bump
01625 599022
www.businessbump.co.uk

Formes
020 8689 1133
www.formes.com
See advert on page 89

From Here to Maternity
www.fromheretomaternity.com

Great Expectations
020 7581 4886

JoJo Maman Bebe
020 7924 6844
www.jojomamanbebe.co.uk

NCT (Maternity Sales) Ltd
0141 636 0600
www.nctms.co.uk

Next
08456 100 500
www.next.co.uk

Nine over Twelve
020 7978 5835
www.nineovertwelve.co.uk

Precious Cargo
01706 626009

The Secret Garden Maternity Wear
01606 738302

www.swells.co.uk
01949 850263

Upfront Maternity Wear
0870 513 4317
www.upfrontmaternity.com

maternity wear: retail

Mothercare branches in most high streets.

N8
Gooseberry Bush
15 Park Road. 020 8342 9898
gberrybush@aol.com

NW3
Formes
66 Rosslyn Hill, Hampstead. 020 7431 7770
www.formes.com

NW11
JoJo Maman Bébé
3 Ashbourne Parade, 1259 Finchley Road.
020 8731 8961
Also baby and children's clothing

SE21
Maternus
33 Dulwich Village. 020 8299 6761
www.maternus.co.uk

SW15
Bumpsadaisy
157 Lower Richmond Road. 020 8789 0329

SW18
Bumpstart
119 Revelstoke Road, Wimbledon Park.
020 8879 3467

SW3
Formes
313 Brompton Road. 020 7584 3337

Great Expectations
78 Fulham Road. 020 7581 4886

Maman
79 Walton Street. 020 7589 8414

SW6
Baby List Company
The Broomhouse, 50 Sulivan Road.
020 7371 5145
See advert on page 149

Blooming Marvellous
725 Fulham Road. 020 7371 0500
Also clothing, nursery products.
See advert on page 87

FoRMES

COLLECTION FOR PREGNANT WOMEN

listen to your feelings

FORMES Boutiques:

LONDON SW3
LONDON W1
LONDON WC2
LONDON NW3
BELFAST
CHELTENHAM
EDINBURGH
GLASGOW
GUILDFORD
LEEDS
MANCHESTER
NOTTINGHAM

DUBLIN
CORK

PARIS 2nd
PARIS 6th
PARIS 16th
NEUILLY S/SEINE
ST GERMAIN EN LAYE
BORDEAUX
CAEN
DIJON
GRENOBLE
LILLE
LIMOGES
LYON 2nd
MARSEILLE 1st
METZ
MONTPELLIER
NANCY
NANTES
NICE
REIMS
RENNES
ROUEN
STRASBOURG
TOULOUSE
TOURS

GENEVA

BRUSSELS
ANTWERP

MADRID
BARCELONA

LISBON

AMSTERDAM

COPENHAGEN

STOCKHOLM

HELSINKI

TEL AVIV

MONTREAL
TORONTO
VANCOUVER

HONG KONG
KOWLOON

TAIPEI

TOKYO SHIBUYA
TOKYO GINZA
FUKUOKA

Daniel Boulton

FoRMES
PARIS

COLLECTION FEMME ENCEINTE

The boutiques: 101 styles in 259 versions in the 59 FORMES boutiques • Addresses in London : 313 Brompton Road, South Kensington • 33 Brook Street, West End • 28 Henrietta Street, Covent Garden • 66 Rosslyn Hill, Hampstead • **The catalogue:** Free catalogue by request on 020 8689 1122, fax 020 8689 2233, e-mail formes@compuserve.com • **The website:** www.formes.com

Suits - Trousers

Leggings - Miniskirts - Dresses - Skirts

Weddings - Parties - Evening Gowns

MUMS 2 BE

For all your fashion needs
during pregnancy, from
Business wear to Leisure wear.

Petite Collection available.
Evening Wear Hire.
Bra fitting & Alteration service.

Mon-Sat 10am-5.30pm

⊖ Kew Gardens
Easy parking at rear of shop

3 Mortlake Terrace, Mortlake Road,
Kew, Richmond, Surrey TW9 3DT

020 8332 6506

Blouses - Jumpers - Jeans

m

maternity wear: retail (cont.)

TW9
Mums 2 Be
3 Mortlake Terrace, Mortlake Road, Kew,
Richmond. 020 8332 6506

W1
Formes
33 Brook Street. 020 7493 2783
See advert on page 89

WC2
Bumpsadaisy
43 The Market, Covent Garden.
020 7379 9831

Formes
28 Henrietta Street. 020 7240 4777
See advert on page 89

mathematics

Kumon Educational
0800 854 714
www.kumon.co.uk
See advert on page 92

medical advice

**Nannyboard - the emergency
organiser**
64 Ellerby Street, London SW6.
020 8741 2369
www.childalert.co.uk
See advert under nanny advice

Doctorcall
43 Hans Place, SW3. 07000 372255

Medipac
020 7350 2079
www.e-med.co.uk

The Gynae Centre
93 Harley Street, W1. 020 7935 7525
www.gynae-centre.co.uk

SOS Doctors Direct
SOS House, 73-77 Britannia Road, SW6.
020 7603 3332

meditation

W4
Calm for Kids
020 8994 5093
calmforkids@aol.com

Please say you saw the ad in
The London Baby Directory

www.BABYdirectory.com Check us out

midwives, independent

(see also antenatal support and information, maternity nannies)

Independent Midwives' Association
1 The Great Quarry, Guildford, Surrey.
01483 821104
www.independentmidwives.org.uk

E3
Ali Herron
020 8983 3617

NE
Lucyann Ashdown
020 7682 0658

SE19
Birth Rites Midwifery Practice
94 Auckland Road, Upper Norwood.
020 8771 7143

SW8
Caroline Flint Midwifery Services
34 Elm Quay Court, Nine Elms Lane,
Vauxhall. 020 7498 2322
midwifecf@aol.com
www.birthcentre.com

W1
Zita West
020 7467 8475
www.zitawest.com
See advert on page 154

W1
London Midwifery Practice
68 Gloucester Place. 020 7486 3123

model agencies

SE1
Childsplay
1 Cathedral Street. 020 7403 4834

E1
Pollyanna Children's Training Theatre
Metropolitan Wharf, Wapping Wall.
020 7702 1937
3-20yrs

SE5
Kids Plus
54 Grove Park. 020 7737 3901

W5
Bubblegum
Ealing Film Studios, Ealing Green.
020 8758 8678
bubblegummodels@aol.com
0-15yrs

W6
Little Acorns
London House, 271-273 King Street.
020 8563 0773
www.littleacorns.co.uk

mother & baby groups

These are usually for mothers with small babies (pre-crawling) and are often run by the local clinic. The National Childbirth Trust runs groups in people's homes in some areas *(see postnatal support and information)*. Other useful sources of information are health visitors, clinics and your local library. For older children, *(see parent & toddler groups, playgroups)*.

Ealing 135 Group
PO Box 135, London W5 1FN
020 8567 8597
www.ealing135.org.uk

mother's helps

(see also au pair agencies, nanny agencies)

More than a cleaner but less than a nanny.

murals & painted nursery furniture

(see also nursery furniture & decor, nursery goods)

E.L.J Design
07958 646 113
emma@vanklaveren.freeserve.co.uk
www.eljdesign.co.uk

Cow Jumped over the Moon
020 8883 0888
cow@lepard.fsnet.co.uk

Monica Janssens
07961 341894
monica@talk21.com

Yoyo Murals
020 8563 2935 www.yoyomurals.com

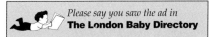
Please say you saw the ad in
The London Baby Directory

museums

(see also outings)

E2
Bethnal Green Museum of Childhood
Cambridge Heath Road. 020 8980 2415
Closed Fri. Mon-Sat 10-5.50pm;
Sun 2.30-5.50pm

Geffrye Museum
Kingsland Road. 020 7739 9893
Tues-Sat 10-5pm; Sun 2-5pm

E3
Ragged School Museum
46-50 Copperfield Road. 020 8980 6405
www.raggedschooolmuseum.org.uk
Free. Wed + Thurs 10-5pm, first Sun of each
month 2-5pm. First Sun of month, family
activities.

EC2
Museum of London
150 London Wall. 020 7600 3699
www.museumoflondon.org.uk
Mon-Sat 10-5.50pm; Sun 12-5.50pm

NW3
London International Gallery of Children's Art
02 Centre, 255 Finchley Road. 020 435 0903
www.ligca.org
Gallery exhibiting children's art.
Workshops

NW9
Royal Air Force Museum
Grahame Park Way, Hendon. 020 8205 2266
Mon-Sun 10-6pm

SE1
Tate Modern
Bankside. 020 7887 8687
www.tate.org.uk
Excellent

Imperial War Museum
Lambeth Road. 020 7416 5000

SE10
National Maritime Museum
Romney Park Road, Greenwich.
020 8858 4422
www.nmm.sc.uk

SE15
Livesey Museum for Children
682 Old Kent Road, Peckham. 020 7639 5604
Under 5s mornings Thurs 10am-12pm

SE17
Cuming Museum
155-157 Walworth Road. 020 7701 1342

SE23
Horniman Museum and Gardens
100 London Road, Forest Hill. 020 8699 1872
www.horniman.demon.co.uk
Free. Mon-Sat 10.30-5.30pm; Sun 2-5.30pm

SW1
Tate Britain
Millbank. 020 7887 8000
www.tate.org.uk
Mon-Sat 10-5.50pm; Sun 2-5.50pm

SW3
National Army Museum
Royal Hospital Road. 020 7730 0717
www.national-army-museum.ac.uk

SW7
Natural History Museum
Cromwell Road. 020 7942 5000
www.nhm.ac.uk
Mon-Sat, 10-5.50pm; Sun 11-5.50pm

Science Museum
Exhibition Road. 020 7938 8008
Mon-Sat 10-6pm; Sun 11-6pm. New
Wellcome Wing includes Launch Pad.
Imax cinema

Victoria and Albert Museum
Cromwell Road. 020 7938 8500
Children free. Mon Sat 10-5.15pm.
Sun 11-5.15pm. Tube to South Kensington

W1
Pollock's Toy Museum
1 Scala Street. 020 7636 3452
toymuseum@hotmail.com
www.pollock.cwc.net
Mon-Sat 10-5pm

Wallace Collection
Hertford House, Manchester Square.
020 7935 0687
No buggies. Free

W3
Gunnersbury Park Museum
Gunnersbury Park, Popes Lane.
020 8992 1612. Excellent local museum

W8
Commonwealth Institute
Kensington High Street. 020 7603 4535

WC1
British Museum
Great Russell Street. 020 7636 1555
Mon-Sat 10-5pm; Sun 10-5.30pm

WC2
London Transport Museum
The Piazza, Covent Garden. 020 7565 7299
www.ltmuseum.co.uk
Mon-Sun, 10-6pm

National Gallery
Trafalgar Square. 020 7839 3321
Free. Mon-Sat, 10-6pm; Wed 10-9pm:
Sun 12-6pm. Quizzes, etc

Somerset House
Courtauld Institute and Gilbert Gallery.
020 7848 2526. Family trails, fountains, etc

music

(see also art, dance, drama)

Throughout London
Monkey Music
01582 766464
www.monkeymusic.co.uk
London and SE

Gymboree Play and Music
0800 092 0911
www.gymboreePlayUK.com
Newborn +

Da Capo
in partnership with Trinity College of
Music. 020 8371 0302
admin@dacapo.co.uk
3-7yrs

Tiny Beats
020 7207 5501

music (cont.)

NW5
Musical Gift Catalogue
51 Fortess Road. 08700 797 797
www.musicalgift.com
Also piano rental

E8/N1/N5/N6/N7/N8/N10/N16/N19/
Rucksack Music Inc
020 8806 9335

North
Colourstrings Music Kindergarten
020 8340 4534

N1
Sumics
Unity Church Hall, Upper Street.
020 7359 3733
5yrs+

Tick Tock
020 7359 9495

N3
Children's Music Box
020 8445 9433

Monica Weil's Creative Music
020 8693 2051
2yrs+

SW3
Music for the Young
St Luke's Church, Sydney Street.
020 7582 8122

SW3/SW11/SW13/SW15
Bea's Baby Music School
020 7228 0904
6mths+

SW3/SW4/SW15/W6
Blueberry Playsongs
Clapham, Putney, Chelsea, Hammersmith.
020 8677 6871
www.blueberry.clara.co.uk
9mths+

SW4/SW8
Music Makers
020 7587 1560

SW6
London Suzuki Group
96 Farm Lane. 020 7386 8006

SW7
The Music House
020 8932 2652

SW11
Music and Piano
020 7350 1303
4yrs+

Tin Pan Annie
Broomwood Methodist Church,
Kyrle Road. 020 8670 0644
Also parties

The Acting Factory
BAC Lavender Hill. 020 7223 2223
mailbox@bac.org.uk

SW11/SW12/SW16/SW18
Mini Music
020 8673 5047
3mths+

SW12
Baby Music Classes
The Art of Health and Yoga,
280 Balham High Road. 020 8682 1800

N3/NW7
Musical Minis
020 8868 0001

N5/NW3, also Enfield, Barnet,
Walthamstow
Tuneful Tots
020 8447 3795

N10/NW3
Crotchets and Quavers
020 8883 2076

NW11
Youth Music Centre
Bigwood House, Bigwood Road.
020 8343 1940
3yrs+

NW7
Adventures in Music
020 8958 2417

NW8
Fun with Music
2 Queensmead, St John's Wood Park.
020 7722 9828

NW8/SW3/W8
Tafelmusik
020 7794 3048

South
Colourstrings Music Kindergarten
020 8547 3073

SE
Music for Little People
020 8852 0118
0-5yrs

SE3
Hickory Jig
St James Church Hall,
Kidbrooke Park Road. 07966 454098
Under 5s

Blackheath Conservatoire of Music
and the Arts
19-21 Lee Road. 020 8852 0234

SE24
Whippersnappers
Brockwell Lido, Dulwich Road.
020 7738 6633

SE26
Mini Maestros
020 8333 0080

the
Music House
for Children
www.musichouseuk.com

INSTRUMENTAL TUITION
Highly qualified teachers carefully chosen for
teaching children from beginners to Grade 8.
Lessons take place after school at the pupil's home.
Tuition provided for: Piano, violin, cello,
flute, clarinet, guitar, trumpet, Saxophone.
Many other instruments also available.

MUSIC & MOVEMENT
Under fives
Develops listening and physical skills.
Accompanied by piano and percussion.
Classes in Notting Hill, Kensington, Shepherds Bush

CHILDREN'S MUSICAL BIRTHDAY PARTIES
All Enquiries call: **020 8932 2652**

Funky Monkey Keyboard Classes
020 8675 8238
5-12yrs

SW13/SW15/SW19
Clapham Tafelmusik
020 8542 8586
3yrs+

SW14
Music Corner
020 8748 1580

Mummy & Me
Studioflex, 26 Priests Bridge. 020 8878 0556

SW16
Smiley Faces Music Club
020 8679 0387

SW19/SW20
Musical Express
020 8946 6043

TW8
Pandemonium
Waterman's Art Centre, 40 High Street.
020 8847 5651

Music & Movement

for Children aged between 9 months - 3¹/₂ years

Classes held at:

Chiswick Town Hall, Heathfield Terrace, W4
Mon & Fri mornings £4 per child or £6 per family
The Priory Community Centre, Acton Lane, W3
Tues & Thus mornings £3.50 per child or £6 per family

Amanda's

Action

Kids

No need to book. Just turn up

Contact Amanda on
020 8933 1269

We also do Fab "Birthday Parties"

Cadenza

Music & Movement

for children under 5 years with
Helen Smith ARCM

Puppets, instruments, tapes & more.
Repertoire changes to maintain interest

No need to book just turn up

£3.50 per session, £2 for siblings
Contact Helen Smith

020 8567 9297

Ealing	
Town Hall Uxbridge Road	**Chiswick**
New Broadway	Bob's Studious Studio
Ealing W5 2BY	Bath Road
Tuesday 10am, 11am	(Corner of Rupert Road)
Wednesday 9.30am	W4
Thursday 10am, 11am, 2pm	**Tuesday 1.30pm**

music (cont.)

W2
Colourstrings Music Kindergarten
020 8948 2066

W3/W4/W5
Amanda's Action Kids 020 8933 1269
actionkids@x-stream.co.uk
9mths-3¹/₂yrs

W4
Music Time
020 8979 8923

Arts Educational Schools
14 Bath Road. 020 8987 6666

W4/W5
Cadenza
020 8567 9297
helen@banjo34.freeserve.co.uk

W5
135 Action Songs & Rhymes
020 8992 7572

Ealing YMCA
25 St Mary's Road. 020 8799 4800

Metro-Gnomes
Pitshanger Methodist Church,
Pitshanger Lane. 020 8932 0654
3yrs+

Music and Song for Tiny Tots
Pitshanger Methodist Church Hall,
Pitshanger Lane. 020 8997 4413

W6
Lotte Moore
020 8748 4823

Louisa Harmer
020 7603 3602

W7
Crackerjack
99 Oaklands Road. 020 8840 3355

W8
The Music House
020 8932 2652
See advert on page 97

W10/NW3
Tafelmusik
020 7794 3048

W13
SNIPS Music & Movement
The Crypt, St John's Church, Mattock Lane.
020 8579 0791

W14
Music for Toddlers
Applegarth Studio, Augustine Road.
020 7603 3602

Please say you saw the ad in
The London Baby Directory

name tapes

Easy2Name
01635 298326
www.easy2name.com

Namemark
01425 277776
www.namemark.co.uk

Simply Stuck
01264 350788
www.simplystuck.com

naming ceremonies

(see also registration of births)

Alternative Ceremonies
01932 862116
www.ceremony.org.uk

Baby Naming Society
Yeoman's Cottage, Kerswell Green,
Kempsey, Worcestershire.
01905 371070

British Humanist Association
47 Theobald's Road, London WC1.
020 7430 0908
National helpline: 0990 168122

nanny advice

Nannyboard - the emergency organiser
64 Ellerby Street, London SW6.
020 8741 2369
www.childalert.co.uk

Please say you saw the ad in
The London Baby Directory

nanny agencies

(see also au pair agencies, babysitters, childcare listings, childminders, maternity nannies, mother's helps)

Baba Walkies
15 Marlborough House, Courtlands, Sheen Road, TW10. 020 8332 1380

Belgravia Nannies
5 Nairn Court, 7 Trinity Road, SW19. 020 8540 8375

Eden Nannies
16 Wimpole Street, W1.
020 7299 3311
www.eden-nannies.co.uk

Elite Nannies
22 Rowena Crescent, SW11.
020 7801 0061
elite.nannies@virgin.net

Advice on choosing a nanny

EDEN
NANNIES

'A personal childcare service for professionals sourcing high calibre nannies and maternity nurses'

We provide:　　**Maternity Nurses**: *Live in/Live out/Nights only*
　　　　　　　　Nannies: *Live in/Live out*
　　　　　　　　Temporary/part-time
　　　　　　　　Overseas

As London's leading domestic agency, we offer a wide selection of elite nannies. The service we provide is professional, efficient, prompt and is tailor made to meet our client's requirements.

Our consultants visit all clients at home before commencing a nanny search. We will then guide, reassure and support through every aspect of the selection process.

All candidates have a minimum of 2 years experience and are interviewed in person by one of our experienced consultants. We thoroughly vet and check all references prior to registering any candidate.

Check out our website for further information on additional services that we offer.
www.eden-nannies.co.uk

EDEN NANNIES 16 Wimpole Street, London W1G 9SZ
Tel: 020 7299 3311 Fax: 020 7631 1813
e-mail: anne.arthur@eden-nannies.co.uk
enquiries@eden-nannies.co.uk

nanny agencies (cont.)

Europlacements
14 Bourne Court, Southend Road,
Woodford Green. 020 8551 9099
www.europlacements.co.uk

Franglais Nannies
9 Kings Road, Mitcham. 020 8646 7663
Marie-Ange@Franglaisnannies.freeserve.co.uk

Hyde Park International
Belmont House, The Dean, Alresford,
Hampshire. 020 7730 0112

Ideal Nannies
2 St Peters Road, W6. 020 8748 4868
www.idealnannies.com

Kensington Nannies
82 Kensington High Street, W8.
020 7937 2333

nanny agencies (cont.)

Little Gems
28 Ruislip Street, SW17. 020 8682 7656
www.littlegems.org.uk

Little Treasures
10 Aldred Road, West Hampstead, NW6.
020 7916 3786
elizabethedmonds@hotmail.com

London Nanny Company
Collier House, 163-169 Brompton Road,
SW3. 020 7591 4444
www.LondonNannyCompany.co.uk

**Montessori Teachers & Nannies
Employment Agency**
107 Bow Road, Bow, E3. 020 8981 8118

Nannies Incorporated
Room 317 The Linen Hall,
162-168 Regent Street, W1. 020 7437 8989
NanniesInc@aol.com
See advert under maternity nannies

Nannies of St James
Inc St James Baby Register

Est. 1994

Specialists in Recruitment
Nannies - Maternity Nurses

We provide a professional and personal childcare consultancy for
clients in the UK and Overseas looking for top notch nannies.

Tel: +44 (0) 20 7348 6100   Fax: +44 (0) 20 7348 6130
E-mail: nanniesstjames@aol.com
Website: www.nanniesofstjames.com

Montessori Teacher's & Nannies

Employment Agency

Permanent, temporary and overseas
placements

The *only* specialist Agency for
Montessori teachers & nannies

For Independent professional advice

020 8981 8118

montgoverness@aol.com

the Nanny agency

We ...

• meet you and
all our nannies
personally

• check our
nannies'
references and
qualifications

• offer you advice
and guidance

North London

020 8883 3162

www.thenannyagency.co.uk
email: nlondon@thenannyagency.co.uk

nanny agencies (cont.)

Nannies of St James
100 New King's Road, SW6. 020 7610 9240
www.nanniesofstjames.co.uk
See advert on page 105

The Nanny Agency
29 Cranbourne Road, Muswell Hill, N10.
020 8883 3162
nlondon@thenannyagency.co.uk
www.thenannyagency.co.uk
See advert on page 105

The Nanny Service
6 Nottingham Street, W1. 020 7935 3515
www.nannyservice.co.uk
See advert for Childminders under babysitting

www.Needananny.net
0800 956 1212

Night Nannies
3 Kempson Road, SW6. 020 7731 6168

Occasional & Permanent Nannies
2 Cromwell Place, SW7. 020 7225 1555
www.nannyworld.co.uk

Platinum Nanny Services
65 Thurleigh Road, SW12. 020 8673 5771
enquiries@platinumnannyservices.fsnet.co.uk

Special People
Palace For All, Schofield Road, N19.
020 7686 0253
special.people@virgin.net
Specialising in special needs.
See advert under special needs

Swansons
4 Brackley Road, W4. 020 8994 5275

nanny agencies (cont.)

Temporary Nannies
Warehouse Office Suites,
2 Ravensbury Terrace, SW18. 020 8947 3344
www.temporarynannies.com

Tinies International & Central London
351 Fulham Palace Road, SW6.
020 7384 0322
www.tinieschildcare.co.uk

Tinies N.London *(N1-21, NW1-8, E5, E9)*
020 8341 1313

Tinies SE London *(SE2-3, SE6, SE7, SE9, SE12, SE18, SE20, SE25-26, SE28)*
020 8464 3131

Top Notch Nannies
49 Harrington Gardens, SW7. 020 7259 2626

Wimbledon Nannies
First Floor,
184 Copse Hill, SW20. 020 8947 4666
wimbledonnannies@btinternet.com

The Lady Magazine
39-40 Bedford Street, WC2. 020 7379 4717
Traditionally a good place to find a nanny

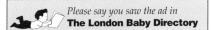

nanny payroll services

(see also financial advice)

Nannies of London Payroll
88 Settrington Road, Fulham,
London SW6 3BA.
020 7371 7094
www.nanny-pay.co.uk

Nanny Payroll Service
Payday Services Ltd, The Studio,
Benefield Road, Brigstock, Kettering.
01536 373 111
www.nannypayroll.co.uk

Please say you saw the ad in
The London Baby Directory

Nanny Payroll Service

Everything necessary is
done to pay your nanny
correctly
We advise and implement
nanny shares
Nationwide service
Fees £98 pa (incl VAT)
The Studio Benefield Road
Brigstock NN14 3ES

Tel: 01536 373111
Fax 01536 373123

www.nannypayroll.co.uk

nanny payroll services (cont.)

Nannytax
PO Box 988, Brighton, BN2 1BY.
01273 626 256
www.nannytax.co.uk

Taxing Nannies
28 Minchenden Crescent, N14.
020 8882 6847

Please say you saw the ad in
The London Baby Directory

nanny share

(see also childcare listings, nanny agencies)

Little Gems
28 Ruislip Street, Tooting, SW17.
020 8682 7656
www.littlegems.org.uk
See advert under nanny agencies

Nanny Share Network
020 8516 5948
www.nannysharenetwork.com

Simply Childcare (ex-The Register)
16 Bushey Hill Road, SE15. 020 7701 6111
www.simplychildcare.com
See advert under childcare listings

SW Nannyshare Register
020 8673 1633

Swansons
4 Brackley Road, W4. 020 8994 5275
See advert under nanny agencies

nappies, cloth & other

Bambino Mio
01604 883777
www.bambino.co.uk

Beaming Baby
0800 0345 672
www.beamingbaby.com

n

nappies, cloth & other (cont.)

BirthWorks
01803 812021
birthworks@thelinhay.freeserve.co.uk

Cotton Bottoms
01798 875300

Eco-Babes
01353 664941
www.ecobabes.freeserve.co.uk

Ellie Pants
0151 200 5012

Green Baby Company
345 Upper Street, London N1. 020 7226 4345
www.greenbabyco.com

Kooshies
0870 607545
www.phpbaby.com

Little Green Earthlets
163 Lower Richmond Road, SW15.
020 8780 3075
See adverton page 111

Modern Baby
01992 505976

Natrababy
01275 371764
www.natracare.com

Real Nappy Association
PO Box 3704, London SE26 4RX.
020 8299 4519
www.realnappy.com
Information on all nappy-related issues

Sam-I-Am
020 8995 9204
www.nappies.net

Snuggle Bums Nappies
020 8361 9087
jnwainer@aol.com

nappy delivery, hire & laundry

Eezy Peezy Cotton Nappy Hire
01959 534207

Food Ferry
020 7498 0827
www.foodferry.com

Nappy Express
128 High Road, Friern Barnet, N11.
020 8361 4040

Nappycare
020 8998 8799
ecmartin@nappycare.co.uk

Number 1s for Nappies
271 Holdbrook Court, Holdbrook South,
Waltham Cross. 01992 713665

West London Real Nappy Nights
020 8568 4913
Ring for details

nature reserves

(see also farms, parks & playgrounds)

E6
East Ham Nature Reserve
Normond Road, East Ham. 020 8470 4525
Largest parish churchyard. 10 acres of
grounds. Visitors' centre with local history,
nature displays, gift shop. Tues-Fri 10-5pm.
Weekends 2-5pm. Free

EN4
Trent Country Park
Cockfosters, Barnet. 020 8449 8706
Cockfosters tube. 413 acres of woodland,
fields and lakes. Pets corner, cafeteria.
Educational walks by arrangement.
7.30am- sunset. Open every day. Free

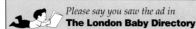

N4
Railway Fields
Green Lanes (entrance opposite Haringey
Green Lanes Station). 020 8348 6005
Phone for opening times. ex-British Rail
goods yard. Woodland, meadows, pond,
playground, Environment Centre. Unique
Haringey Knotweed (!). Summer
playschemes

N5
Gillespie Park
191 Drayton Park. 020 7354 5162
Ponds, meadows, café, Ecology Centre

N11
Coppetts Wood
Colney Hatch Lane, Friern Barnet.

NW1
Camley Street Natural Park
12 Camley Street, Kings Cross.
020 7833 2311
2 acres. Community nature reserve in the
middle of Kings Cross. Mon-Thurs 9-5pm.
Weekends 11-5pm. Closed Friday. Winter
10-4pm. Community and children's events.
Free

NW8
St John's Wood Churchyard
between St John's Wood High Street &
Wellington Road. 020 7641 1548
Open 8am-dusk. Thistle meadow, glade,
wildlife hedge, Senses walk, woodland,
nectar bed, fern and moss area.

SE16
Russia Dock Woodlands
Downtown Road. 020 7277 4068

SE22
Dawson's Hill
Dunstan's Road.
8 acres with activity days

SE23
Horniman Gardens
Horniman Museum and Public Garden
Trust, 100 London Road, Forest Hill.
020 8699 8924
BR to Forest Hill, 10 min walk. 15 Acres,
including 1/4 mile railway line, nature
walks. 7am-dusk. Railway 9am-dusk. Free

SE26
Sydenham Hill Wood
Crescent Wood Road. 020 8699 5698
Largest remaining tract of the old Great
North Wood

SL0
Iver Nature Study Centre
Slough Road, Iver Heath. 01895 270 730
Two acres with three ponds, meadows and
woodland with rabbits. Mini assalt course
for 4-5yrs olds. 9-5.30pm. Winter 9-4pm.
Donation appreciated. A4007, by Mansfield
Farm. Uxbridge tube

SW13
The Wetland Centre
Wildfowl & Wetlands Trust, Queen
Elizabeth Walk. 020 8876 8995
info@wetlandcentre.org.uk
Europe's largest urban wetland - 105 acres
of lakes, ponds and marshes. Over 130
world bird species and a host of other
creatures. Discovery centre, café, etc. Don't
forget your binoculars.

SW18
Wandworth Nature Study Centre
Wandsworth Common, Dorlcote Road.
020 8871 3863

UB
Horsenden Hill
Horsenden Lane North, Perivale.
Open hillside and forest, with good views

Litten Nature Reserve
Greenford Road, Greenford. 020 8578 7650

W4
Gunnersbury Triangle
Bollo Lane (opposite Chiswick Park
Station). 020 8747 3881
Across the road from Chiswick Park tube.
Wed 10-4pm; Fri 1-4pm; Sun 2-4pm. Six
acres of woodland, meadows and pond.
Free

W5
Fox Wood
Fox Lane, Hillcrest Road.
Woodland path, wildflower meadow

HAL'S HOUSE

The Nearly New
Childrenswear & Nursery Store

131 Walham Green Court
Moore Park Road, SW6 2DG

Tel/Fax: 020 7381 6464

e-mail: halshouse@hotmail.com

nearly new equipment, toy & clothing shops

Our website, **www.babydirectory.com** has a direct link to **www.kidskiosk.com**, the online nearly new store.

E5
Merry-Go-Round
12 Clarence Road. 020 8985 6308
peter@twotiger.demon.co.uk

E9
Chocolate Crocodile
39 Morpeth Road, Victoria Park.
020 8985 3330

N6
Rainbow
249 & 253 Archway Road. 020 8340 8003

N8
Totters
57 Tottenham Lane. 020 8341 0377

N16
Encore
53 Stoke Newington Church Street.
020 7254 5329

N17
Simply Outgrown
360 Lordship Lane. 020 8801 0568

NW5
Boomerang
2 Leverton Road. 020 7284 3967

SW6
Hal's House
131 Walham Green Court,
Moore Park Road. 020 7381 6464
halshouse@hotmail.com

SW11
Goodies
52 Webbs Road. 020 7924 2323

SW12
Swallows and Amazons
91 Nightingale Lane, Clapham.
020 8673 0275

SW18
Bunnys
201 Replingham Road, Southfields.
020 8875 1228

SW20
Rocking Horse
600 Kingston Road. 020 8542 4666

W4
Little Trading Company
7 Bedford Corner, The Avenue, Chiswick.
020 8742 3152

Pixies
14 Fauconberg Road. 020 8995 1568
www.pixiesonline.co.uk

W13
Snips
The Crypt, St John's Church, Mattock Lane.
020 8579 0791
Open Tues and Thurs am, first Sat of month

W14
Boomerang
69 Blythe Road. 020 7610 5232

nurseries, private & nursery schools

(see also helplines: education, schools, tuition)

There is an overlap in the field of private childcare provision and education, and many of the terms seem to be interchangeable amongst the providers. These listings include the full gamut, from nurseries to Montessori nurseries, day or daycare nurseries and nursery schools. **Pre-prep schools** (preparing the child for big school, usually at 7 years old) have been listed under the schools section, though they often have a nursery class for 3- or 4-year-olds, and this section should also be consulted. **Prep school** then takes your child through to 11 or 13 by which time you should have well outgrown this book *(see family planning)*.

Babies from 3 months onwards can attend a **nursery** or **day care nursery**, and we have listed those offering a full working day (e.g. 8am-6pm), as "full day" in our listings. In many of these nurseries, older children will graduate from the baby section to a more structured section very like a nursery school, but with longer hours for play, sleep, etc. In general, a **crèche** only offers a few hours of unstructured supervision, while parents do something else *(see health clubs with crèches, shopping crèches)*. At a **playgroup** the carer usually remains in attendance. A **nursery school** for $2^1/2$ to 5 year-olds usually follows a basic school day (9am-3.30pm) and term but pupils may attend only one session, morning or afternoon. Many nurseries use **Montessori** methods, a system devised by Maria Montessori in 1907 which emphasises training of the senses and encouragement rather than a rigid academic curriculum.

For nearly all nurseries and schools in the private sector, early **registration** is recommended, so ring, visit and inform yourself in time, even if you later decide not to pursue that option.

For a list of **state-run** nurseries, or state primary schools with nursery classes attached, contact your Under 8s section at the local council *(see under councils)* or check out www.childcare.gov.uk. For foreign, see under the relevant section. Good luck. You'll need it!

Childcare Link
www.childcarelink.gov.uk
08000 96 02 96

nurseries, private & nursery schools (cont.)

E1
Animal House Nursery (Busy Bees)
69 Royal Mint Square, Cartwright Street.
020 7480 7166
3mths-5yrs. Full day

Buffer Bear at Barts & The London (Whitechapel)
71 Varden Street. 020 7641 4361
3mths-5yrs. Full day

Green Gables Montessori School
St Paul's Institute, 302 The Highway.
020 7488 2374
18mths-5yrs. Full day

Spitalfields Nursery
21 Lamb Street. 020 7375 0775
www.nurseryworks.com
See advert on page 117

E3
Pillar Box Montessori Nursery School
107 Bow Road. 020 8980 0700
0-7yrs. Full day

E4
Amhurst Nursery
13 The Avenue. 020 8527 1614
2-5yrs. Full day

Billet's Corner Nursery (Nursery Works)
adj. Sainsbury's Low Hall Store,
11 Walthamstow Avenue. 020 8523 3823
3mths-5yrs. Full day
www.nurseryworks.com
See advert on page 117

Chingford Activity Nursery
22 Marborough Road, Chingford.
020 8527 2902
0-5yrs. Full day

Chingford Childrens Day Centre
Titley Close. 020 8529 4067
6mths-5yrs. Full day

College Gardens Nursery School
College Gardens. 020 8529 3885
3-5yrs

Handsworth Avenue Childrens Day Centre
32 Handsworth Avenue. 020 8527 5364
6mths-5yrs. Full day

Merryfield Montessori Nursery
76 Station Road, Chingford. 020 8524 7697
2-5yrs. Full day

Rocking Horse Nursery
1 Hatch Lane. 020 8523 7030
1-5yrs. Full day

E8
Independent Place Nursery
Units 26/27 Independent Place,
The Forum, Shacklewell Lane.
020 7275 7755
6mths-5yrs. Full day

E11
Acacia Nursery
Cecil Road. 020 8558 4444

Humpty Dumpty Nursery
24/26 Fairlop Road, Leytonstone.
020 8539 3810
1-5yrs. Full day

Just Learning Nursery
Whipps Cross Hospital,
Whipps Cross Road. 020 8988 0818

E13
Stepping Stones Childcare
Woodside School, Woodside Road.
020 7476 8321
3mths-5yrs. Full day, termtime only

E14
Bushytails Private Day Nursery/Nursery School
519 Glen Terrace, 591 Manchester Road.
020 7537 7776
0-5yrs. Full day

Unicorn Day Nursery
13 Columbus Courtyard, Canary Wharf.
020 7513 0505
3mths-5yrs. Full day

E15
Stepping Stones Childcare
Brickfields Centre, Welfare Road.
020 8534 8777
6mths-5yrs. Full day

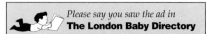
Please say you saw the ad in **The London Baby Directory**

n

THE PLACE TO LEARN AND GROW

OFSTED Approved Montessori School
Flexible hours open 7am to 7pm
For ages 3 months-5 years
Superior Babysitting Agency
Organic food provided where possible

Hopes & Dreams Nursery

339-341 CITY ROAD, ISLINGTON,

LONDON, EC1V 1LJ

TEL: 020 7833 9388   FAX: 020 7837 5517

www.hopesanddreams.co.uk

n

nurseries, private & nursery schools (cont.)

E17
Church Hill
Woodbury Road. 020 8520 4919

Just Learning Nursery
20 Sutton Road, Walthamstow.
020 8527 9711

Low Hall
Low Hall Lane. 020 8520 1689

Tom Thumb Nursery
20 Shirley Close, 1-7 Beulah Road.
020 8520 1329
2-5yrs. Full day

EC1
Hopes and Dreams
339-341 City Road. 020 7833 9388

Leapfrog Day Nursery
49 Clifton Street. 020 7422 0088
3mths-5yrs. Full day

HA0
Alperton Nursery (Nursery Works)
c/o Sainsburys's Alperton Store,
360 Ealing Road, Alperton, Wembley.
020 8566 7663. 3mths-5yrs. Full day
www.nurseryworks.com
See advert on page 117

Happy Child Day Nursery
Middlesex House, Northwick Road.
020 8998 4949. 3mths-5yrs. Full day
www.happychild.co.uk
See advert on page 119

N1
Beckett House Montessori Nursery
98 Richmond Avenue. 020 7278 8824
2^1/$_2$-5yrs. Full day

Children's House
77 Elmore Street. 020 7354 2113
2^1/$_2$-5yrs

Floral Place Nursery (Nursery Works)
2 Floral Place, Northampton Grove.
020 7354 9945
3mths-5yrs. Full day
www.nurseryworks.com
See advert on page 117

The Grove Pre-School & Nursery
3 Shepperton House, 91 Shepperton Road.
020 7226 4037
3mths-5yrs. Full day

Mace Montessori Nursery
327 Upper Street. 020 7704 2805
2-5yrs. Full day

Rosemary Works Early Years Centre
Unit 2a, Branch Place. 020 7613 5500
3mths-3yrs. Full day

St Andrew's Montessori
St Andrew's Church, Thornhill Square.
020 7700 2961
3-5yrs

N2
Annemount School
18 Holne Chase. 020 8455 2132
2^1/$_2$-7yrs

Fortis Green Nursery
70 Fortis Green. 020 8883 1266
6mths-5yrs. Full day

Excellent children's day nurseries providing quality education and care for children from 3 months to 5 years. Qualified staff to cater for all your child's needs.

Full time or part time places available all year round.

Nurseries in Acton, Alperton, Ealing, Harlesden, Kilburn, Northfields, Perivale and Queens Park.

For further details, please call Happy Child Head Office
Tel: **020 8579 8558**
or visit our website at **www.happychild.co.uk**

N3
Pentland Nursery (Nursery Works)
224 Squires Lane, Finchley. 020 8970 2441
3mths-5yrs. www.nurseryworks.com
See advert on page 117

N4
Asquith Court Finsbury Park
Dulas Street, Islington. 020 7263 3090
3mths-5yrs. Full day
See advert on page 125

Crouch Hill Day Nursery
33 Crouch Hill. 020 7561 1533
3mths-5yrs. Full day

Holly Park Montessori
Holly Park Methodist Church Hall,
Crouch Hill. 020 7263 6563
2-11yrs

Little Jewel Pre School
St Paul's Church Hall, Cavendish Road.
020 8341 27433
18mths-5yrs. Full day

North London Rudolf Steiner School
Holy Trinity Church Hall,
Stapleton Hall Road. 020 8986 8968
Address for post: 89 Blurton Road, E5 0NH.
$2^{1}/_{2}$-7yrs.
Also parent & toddler, etc for babies

N5
Little Angels Private Day Nursery
217 Blackstock Road. 020 7354 5070
3mths-4yrs. Full day

New Park Montessori School & Nursery
67 Highbury New Park. 020 7226 1109
4mths-6yrs

N6
Avenue Nursery School
2 Highgate Avenue. 020 8348 6815
$2^{1}/_{2}$-$5^{1}/_{2}$yrs

Highgate Activity Nursery
1 Church Road. 020 8348 9248

Ladybird Montessori
The Scout Hall, Sheldon Avenue.
020 7586 0740
$2^{1}/_{2}$-5yrs. Mornings

nurseries, private & nursery schools (cont.)

Rainbow Montessori
Highgate United Reform Church,
Pond Square. 020 7328 8986
2¹/₂-5yrs

N7

Gower School
18 North Road. 020 7700 2445
3mths-5yrs

Kids Unlimited@Mary Seacole Nursery
Camden & Islington Health Authority,
Tollington Way. 020 7281 6712
3mths-5yrs. Full day

Sam Morris Centre Nursery
Parkside Crescent, Isledon Road.
020 7609 1735
6mths-5yrs. Full day

N8

Adventure Land Day Nursery
18 Gisburn Road. 020 8347 6951
2¹/₂-5yrs. Full day

Ark Montessori Nursery School
42 Turnpike Lane, Hornsey. 020 8881 6556
2-5yrs. Full day

Claremont Day Nursery
7 Harold Road. 020 8340 3841
2-5yrs. Full day

Hollybush Nursery
5 Redston Road. 020 8348 8537
2-5yrs. Full day

Little Tree Montessori
143 Ferme Park Road. 020 8342 9231
2¹/₂-5yrs

Playland Day Nursery
40 Tottenham Lane. 020 8341 5199
2-5yrs

Ruff 'N' Tumble
51 Crouch Hall Road. 020 8348 2469
2-5yrs. Full day

Starshine Nursery
Hornsey Club, Tivoli Road. 020 8348 9909
2-5yrs

N9

Blossoms
85 Bounces Road. 020 8351 0874

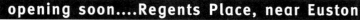

Edmonton Community Day Nursery
24 Cyprus Road. 020 8807 9649
2¹/₂-5yrs. Full day

New Horizons Nursery
Walbrook House, 1 Huntingdon Road.
020 8351 8280
2-5yrs. Full day

Rainbow Nursery Firs Farm
1-4 Kipling Terrace, Great Cambridge Road.
020 8807 9078
2¹/₂-5yrs

Tara Kindergarten
310-314 Hartford Road. 020 8804 4484
3mths-5yrs. Full day

N10
3-4-5 Pre-School
Friends Meeting House, Church Crescent.
07966 541889
2¹/₂-5yrs

3-4-5 Pre-School
Tetherdown Hall, United Reform Church,
Tetherdown. 020 8883 1902
2¹/₂-3yrs

Grey Gates Nursery
182 Muswell Hill Road. 020 8883 5640
6mths-5yrs. Full day

Montessori House
5 Princes Avenue. 020 8444 4399
2-5yrs. Full day

Nursery Montessori
24 Tetherdown, Muswell Hill.
020 8883 7958
2-5yrs. Full day

Rosemount Nursery School
6 Grosvenor Road, Muswell Hill.
020 8883 5842
2-5yrs. Full day

N12
Finchley Nursery
c/o David Lloyd Leisure, Leisure Way,
Finchley High Road. 020 8343 8500
Part of Busy Bees

N14
Salcombe Pre-School (Asquith Court Schools)
33 The Green, Southgate. 020 8882 2136
2-5yrs. Full day
See advert on page 125

Shining Eyes & Busy Minds Pre-School
West Grove Primary School, Chase Road.
020 8350 4584
2-5yrs. Full day

Southgate Day Nursery
25 Oakwood Avenue. 020 8886 2824
3mths-5yrs. Full day

Wonderland Day Nursery
2-16 Burleigh Parade, Burleigh Gardens.
020 8886 6163
3mths-5yrs. Full day

N15
Sugar Plum Nursery
255 West Green Road. 020 8800 7560
2-5yrs. Full day

Under 5s Centre
The Green, Phillips Lane. 020 8808 9194
2-5yrs. Full day

N16
Coconut Nursery
133 Stoke Newington Church Street.
020 7923 0720
2-5yrs

Sunrise Nursery
1 Cazenove Road. 020 8806 6279
2-4¹/₂yrs. Full day

Thumbelina Nursery
169-171 Green Lanes. 020 7354 1278
2-5yrs

N17
Blossoms Nursery
Unit 10, Imperial House. 020 8808 0178
2-5yrs. Full day

Penn Nursery
33 Forester Road. 020 8808 7373
2-5yrs. Full day

Sunrise Nursery
55 Coniston Road. 020 8885 3354
30mths-4yrs. Not subject to Social Services Inspection

N18
Ashland Private Day Nursery
36 Weir Hall Road. 020 8345 5752
2-5yrs

nurseries, private & nursery schools (cont.)

Tinkerbells Nursery
2 Amersham Avenue. 020 8372 7682
0-5yrs. Full day

N19
Chameleon Nursery
76 Dartmouth Park Hill. 020 7272 9111
3mths-5yrs. Full day

Montpelier Nursery
115 Brecknock Road. 020 7485 9813
3-5yrs. Full day

N21
Bumble Bees Montessori Day Nursery
8 Uplands Way, Winchmore Hill.
020 8364 3647. 2-5yrs

Highfields Day Nursery
698 Green Lanes. 020 8360 6101
2-5yrs. Full day

Teddys Day Nursery
18 Green Dragon Lane. 020 8364 3842
3mths-5yrs. Full day

Woodberry Day Nursery (Child Base)
63 Church Hill, Winchmore Hill.
020 8882 6917

N22
3-4-5 Pre-School
c/o The Actual Workshop, The Grove,
Alexandra Park. 07778 739 319
2¹/2-5yrs

Alexandra Nursery School
189 Alexandra Park Road. 020 8374 9492
2-5yrs

Bowes Park Nursery
63-65 Whittington Road. 020 8888 1142
1-5yrs. Full day

Kids Business
New River Sports Centre, White Hart Lane.
020 8881 5738
2-5yrs. Full day

Rainbow Corner Nursery
24 Elgin Road. 020 8888 5862
2-5yrs. Full day

NW1
Agar Community Nursery
Wrotham Road. 020 7485 5195
2-5yrs. Full day

Alpha Beta Nursery
16 Kentish Town Road. 020 7482 2263

Camden Day Nursery (Bringing Up Baby)
123-127 St Pancras Way. 020 7284 3600
6mths-3yrs. Full day
www.bringingupbaby.co.uk
See advert on page 123

Dolphin Montessori School
Luther Tyndale Church Hall,
Leighton Crescent. 020 7267 3994
2¹/2-4¹/2yrs

St Mark's Square Nursery School
St Mark's Church, St Mark's Square.
020 7586 8383
2-5yrs. Full day

NW2
Fordwych Nursery
107 Fordwych Road. 020 8208 2591
2-5yrs

The Little Ark Montessori Nursery School
80 Westbere Road. 020 7794 6359
2-5yrs. Full day

Montessori Nursery School
St Cuthberts Church, Fordwych Road.
020 8209 0813
2¹/2-5yrs

Neasden Montessori
St Catherine's Church Hall, Dudden Hill
Lane. 020 8208 1631
2-5yrs

NW3
Belsize Square Synagogue Nursery School
51 Belsize Square. 020 7431 3823
2¹/2-5yrs co-ed

Chalcot Montessori School
9 Chalcot Gardens. 020 7722 1386

Cherryfields Preschool Nursery
523 Finchley Road. 020 7431 0055
2-5yrs

n

bringing up baby
www.bringingupbaby.co.uk

With our strong educational programmes and high calibre staff, we offer your child the best start in life.

Day Nursery provision for 3 month to 5 year olds

Quality education and care for your child

Qualified staff to meet all emotional/social needs

Varied and stimulating curriculum

Safe, welcoming, child-friendly premises

Open minimum 50 weeks, 10 hour days

Nurseries in Brentford, Wembley, Hammersmith, Shepherd's Bush and Camden.

FOR FURTHER INFORMATION:
tel: 020 7738 0160
or e-mail: office@bringingupbaby.co.uk

INVESTOR IN PEOPLE

n

nurseries, private & nursery schools (cont.)

Church Row Nursery
Crypt Room, Hampstead Parish Church,
Church Row. 020 7431 2603
2-5yrs

Eton Nursery Montessori School
45 Buckland Crescent. 020 7722 1532
2-5yrs. Full day

Hampstead Hill Nursery School
St. Stephens Hall, Pond Street.
020 7435 6262
2-5yrs. Full day

Hilltop Nursery School
Christchurch, Hampstead Square.
020 8455 2132
$2^1/_2$-5yrs

Leaps & Bounds
02 Centre, Finchley Road. 0800 371171
3mths-5yrs. Full day

Maria Montessori Children's House
26 Lyndhurst Gardens. 020 7435 3646
$2^1/_2$-6yrs. Full day.
www.montessori-ami.org

North Bridge House Stepping Stone School
33 Fitzjohn's Avenue. 020 7435 9641
$2^1/_2$-5yrs

Oak Tree Nursery
69 Fitzjohn's Avenue. 020 7435 1916
$2^1/_2$-11yrs (girls) - 13yrs (boys). Part of
Devonshire House School.

Octagon Nursery School
Saint Saviour's Church Hall, Eton Road.
020 7586 3206
$2^1/_2$-5yrs

Olivers Montessori Nursery School
52 Belsize Square. 020 7435 5898
2-5yrs

Peter Piper Nursery School
St Luke's Church Hall, Kidderpore Avenue.
020 7431 7402
2-4yrs

Primrose Nursery (Rudolph Steiner)
32 Glenilla Road. 020 7794 5865
3-5yrs

Ready, Steady, Go
12a King Henry's Road. 020 7586 6289
$2^1/_2$-5yrs

NW4
Asquith Court Hill Park
5 Sunningfields Road, Hendon.
020 8201 5817
18mths-5yrs. Full day
See advert on page 125

Asquith Court Nursery (Hendon)
46 Allington Road. 020 8203 9020
18mths-5yrs. Full day
See advert on page 125

NW5
Bluebells Nursery
Our Lady Help of Christians Church Hall,
Lady Margaret Road. 020 7284 3952
$2^1/_2$-5yrs

Chaston Place Nursery
Chaston Place, off Grafton Terrace.
020 7482 0701
3mths-7yrs. Full day

Cresswood Nursery
215 Queen's Crescent. 020 7485 1551
2-5yrs. Full day

Highgate Children's Centre (part of Nursery Works)
Highgate Studios, 53-79 Highgate Road.
3mths-5yrs. Also after school & holiday
clubs for 4-10yrs. www.nurseryworks.com
See advert on page 117

Rooftops Nursery
Priestley House, Athlone Street.
020 7267 7949
2-4yrs. Full day

Truro Street Nursery
7-12 Truro Street. 020 7485 0276
$2^1/_2$-5yrs

York Rise Nursery
St Mary Brookfield Church Hall,
York Rise. 020 7485 7962
2-5yrs. Full day

NW6
Beehive Montessori
147 Chevening Road. 020 8969 2235
2-5yrs. Full day

Chaston Nursery School
30-31 Palmerston Road. 020 7372 2120
3mths-5yrs. Full day

ASQUITH COURT NURSERIES

PROVIDING EXCELLENCE IN COMBINED EARLY YEARS LEARNING AND CHILDCARE FOR THE UNDER 5s

Open from 8.00am-6.00pm every weekday throughout the year

For a site near you and further details, please call:

Freephone
0800 591 875

Web site address: www.asquithcourt.co.uk

nurseries, private & nursery schools (cont.)

Happy Child
St Anne's & St Andrew's Church Hall,
125 Salusbury Road. 020 7625 1966
2-5yrs. Full day. www.happychild.co.uk
See advert on page 119

Happy Child Day Nursery
2 Victoria Road. 020 7328 8791
3mths-5yrs. www.happychild.co.uk
See advert on page 119

The Learning Tree Nursery
Quex Road, Methodist Church.
020 7372 7213
2¹/₂-5yrs

Mackenzie Day Nursery
St Mary's Church Hall, Abbey Road.
020 7624 0370
2-5yrs. Full day

Rainbow Montessori School (Sherriff Road)
St James's Hall, Sherriff Road.
020 7328 8986
2¹/₂-5yrs

Sington Nursery
Portakabins Community Centre,
160 Mill Lane. 020 7431 1279
3-5yrs. Full day

Teddies
2 West End Lane. 020 7372 3290
3mths-5yrs. Full day
www.teddiesnurseries.co.uk
See advert on page 135

West Hampstead Pre-School (Asquith Court School)
11 Woodchurch Road. 020 7328 4787
18mths-5yrs. Full day *See advert on page 125*

NW8

Buffer Bear at Westminster/Carlton Hill Nursery
86 Carlton Hill. 020 7641 4491
6mths-5yrs. Full day

St John's Wood Synagogue Kindergarten
37/41 Grove End Road. 020 7286 3859
2-5yrs

Toddler's Inn Nursery School
Cicely Davies Hall, Cochrane Street.
020 7586 0520. 2-5yrs. Full day

NW9

Gower House School & Nursery
Blackbird Hill. 020 8205 2509
2-11yrs

Joel Nursery
214 Colindeep Lane. 020 8200 0189
2-5yrs. Full day

NW10

Almost Big School
32 Crouch Road. 020 8453 0136
2-4yrs. Full day

Happy Child Day Nursery
15 Longstone Avenue. 020 8961 3485
3mths-5yrs. Full day
www.happychild.co.uk
See advert on page 119

Kindercare Montessori
Bridge Park Sports Centre, Harrow Road.
020 8838 1688
2-5yrs. Full day

NW11

Asquith Court Pre-School, Golders Green
212 Golders Green Road. 020 8458 7388
18mths-5yrs. Full day. *See advert on page 125*

Clowns
153 North End Road, Golders Green.
020 8455 7333
1-5yrs. Full day

Hellenic College Montessori Nursery
Greek Orthodox Cathedral of Holy Cross &
St Michael, The Riding. 020 8455 8511
2¹/₂-5yrs

Hoop Lane Montessori School
31.5 Hoop Lane, Unitarian Church Hall.
020 8209 0813. 2¹/₂-5yrs. Mornings only

Pardes House Kindergarten
Golders Green Synagogue,
41 Dunston Road. 020 8458 4003
2-4yrs. Full day

SE1

Canterbury House Day Nursery (Child Base)
Royal Street. 020 7620 0944

City Creche Daycare
14 Winchester Walk. 020 7403 3604
6mths-3yrs. Full day

Coral Day Nursery
Windmill House, Wootton Street.
020 7928 0597
0-5yrs. Full day

Kintore Way Nursery
Grange Road. 020 7237 1894
3-5yrs. Part & full time

St Patrick's Creche, Nursery and Montessori School
91 Cornwall Road. 020 7928 5557
3mths-5yrs. Full day

Scarecrows Day Nursery
24 Marshalsea Road. 020 7234 0884
5mths-5yrs. Full day

Waterloo Nursery (Nursery Works)
The Chandlery, 50A Westminster Bridge Road. 020 7721 7432
3mths-5yrs. Full day
www.nurseryworks.com
See advert on page117

SE2
Croft Day Nursery
75 Woolwich. 01322 431045
4mths-5yrs. Full day

SE3
Blackheath Day Nursery
The Rectory Field, Charlton Road.
020 8305 2526
6mths-5yrs. Full day

Blackheath High School
Wemyss Road. 020 8852 1537
3-11yrs

Blackheath Nursery and Prep
4 St German Place. 020 8858 0692
3-11yrs

Blackheath Montessori Centre
Independents Road, Blackheath.
020 8852 6765
Co-ed 3-5yrs. Full day

Greenwich Steiner School
3 North Several. 020 8318 7787
3-6^1/2yrs. Mornings

Lingfield Day Nursery
37 Kidbrooke Grove. 020 8858 1388
18mths-5yrs. Full day

SE4
Catherine House Day Nursery
71 Tressillian Road, Brockley. 020 8692 5015
3mths-5yrs. Full day.

Chelwood Nursery School
Chelwood Walk, Turnam Road, Brockley.
020 7639 2514
3-5yrs.

Cherry Li Nursery
40 Tyrwhitt Road, Brockley. 020 8691 0497
2-5yrs. Full day

Dressington Pre-School
30 Rushey Mead, Brockley. 020 8690 9845
2-5yrs. Full day

Hillyfields Day Nursery
41 Harcourt Road, Brockley. 020 8694 1069
2-5yrs. Full day

Lillingtons' Montessori Nursery School
Chudleigh Road, Ladywell. 020 8690 2184
2^1/2-5yrs. Full day

Little Gems
Clare Road, Brockley. 020 8692 0061
2-5yrs. Full day

SE5
Guppies Montessori
Camberwell. 020 7703 9966
2-5yrs. 9-3.30pm

The Nest Playgroup & Pre-School
Longfield Hall, 50 Knatchbull Road.
020 7978 9158
2^1/2-5yrs

Our Precious Ones
Clemance Hall, Brisbane Street,
Camberwell. 020 7701 9857
2-5yrs. Full day

St John's Montessori Nursery
Crawford Tenants Hall, Denmark Road.
020 7737 2123
2-5yrs. Full day

South East Montessori
40 Ivanhoe Road. 020 7737 1719
2-5yrs. Full day

nurseries, private & nursery schools (cont.)

SE6
Little Learners Day Nursery
Rubens Street, Catford. 020 8291 3994
18mths-5yrs. Full day

Thornsbeach Day Nursery
Thornsbeach Road, Catford. 020 8697 7699
2-5yrs. Full day

SE7
Pound Park Nursery School
Pound Park Road, Charlton. 020 8858 1791
3-4^1/2yrs. Part time

SE8
Bunny Hop Day Nursery
1 King Fisher Square, Deptford.
020 8691 7171
2-4^1/2yrs. Full day

Clyde Nursery School
Alverton Street, Deptford. 020 8692 3653
3-5yrs.

Rachel McMillan Nursery School
McMillan Street, Deptford. 020 8692 4041

Rainbow Nursery
44 Alverton Street. 020 8692 1224
2-5yrs. Full day

SE9
Coombe Nursery
467 Footscray Road, New Eltham.
020 8850 4445
2-5yrs. Full day

Elizabeth Terrace Day Nursery
18-22 Elizabeth Terrace, Eltham.
020 8294 0377
4mths-5yrs. Full day

**New Eltham Pre-School & Nursery
(Asquith Court)**
699 Sidcup Road. 020 8851 5057
3mths-5yrs. Full day
See advert on page 125

Willow Park Day Nursery
13 Gleneck Road. 020 8850 8988
2mths-2yrs. Full day

SE10
Mrs Bartlett's Nursery
The Church of the Ascension,
Dartmouth Row. 020 8692 1014
2^1/2-5yrs

Sommerville Day Nursery
East Side Stage, Sparta Street, Groenmich.
020 8691 9080
2-4yrs. Full day

SE11
Ethelred Nursery School
10 Lollard Street. 020 7582 9711
3-4yrs

Toad Hall Nursery School
37 St Mary's Gardens. 020 7735 5087
2mths-5yrs. Full day

Vauxhall Christian Centre Playgroup
Tyers Street, Vauxhall. 020 7582 2618
2^1/2-5^1/2yrs. Mornings

William Wilberforce Day Nursery
Longton House, Lambeth Walk.
020 7735 6317
6mths-5yrs. Full day

SE12
Asquith Court Kidbrooke Park Crèche
Kidbrooke Park Road,
corner of Weigall Road. 020 8856 1328
Full day. *See advert on page 125*

Colfe's Prep School
Hornpark Lane, Lee. 020 8852 2283
3-18yrs. Full day

Grove Park Pre-School
353 Baring Road, Grove Park. 020 8857 8258
3mths-5yrs. Full day

Lingfield Day Nursery
155 Baring Road. 020 8851 7800
18mths-5yrs. Full day

Riverston Prep School
63-69 Eltham Road. 020 8318 4327
1-16yrs. Full day

SE13
The Coach House Montessori
30 Slaithwaite Road, Lewisham.
020 8297 2021
2-5yrs. Full day

Little Gems Day Nursery
Clare Road, Barclay. 020 8692 0061
2-4^1/2yrs. Full day

Mother Goose Nursery
113 Brooke Bank Road. 020 8694 8700
1-5yrs. Full day

Sandrock Day Nursery
10 Sandrock Road. 020 8692 8844
2-5yrs. Full day

Saplings Day Nursery
83a Belmont Hill, Lewisham. 020 8852 8071
4mths-5yrs. Full day

Step by Step Day Nursery
Dindon House, Monument Garden.
020 8297 5070
3mths-5yrs

Village Nursery
St Mary Centre, Ladywell Road, Lewisham.
020 8690 6766
2-5yrs. Full day

SE14
Stars of Hope Nursery
74 Wildgoose Drive. 020 7639 1777
2-5yrs. Full day

Stepping Stones Montessori Nursery
Church of God of Prophecy, Kitto Road.
020 7277 6288
6mths-5yrs. Full day

Woodpecker Early Years
20 Woodpecker Road. 020 8694 9557
2-5yrs. Full day

SE15
Bellenden Day Nursery
198 Bellenden Road. 020 7639 4896
2-5yrs

Colourbox Day Nursery
385 Ivydale Road. 020 7277 9662
6mths-5yrs. Full day

Goslings Day Nursery
106 Evelina Road. 020 7639 5261
6mths-5yrs. Full day

Ladybird Nursery
143 Peckham Rye. 020 7639 5943
2-5yrs. Full day

Mother Goose Nursery
54 Linden Grove, Nunhead. 020 7277 5956
3mths-2yrs. Full day

Mother Goose Nursery
34 Waveney Avenue, Nunhead.
020 7277 5951
18mths-5yrs. Full day

Nell Gwynn Nursery
Meeting Houselane, Peckam. 020 7252 8265
3-5yrs. Full- & part-time places

Peckham Rye Day Nursery
24 Waveney Avenue, Peckham Rye.
020 7635 5501
4mths-5yrs. Full day.

Playaway Dulwich Daycare
385 Ivydale Road, Peckham. 020 7277 9662
6mths-5yrs. Full day

Sankofa Day Nursery
14 Sharratt Street. 020 7277 6243
2-5yrs. Full day

Villa Nursery
54 Lyndhurst Grove. 020 7703 6216
6mths-5yrs. Full day. School opening Sept
5-7yrs

SE16
5 Steps Community Nursery
51-52 Alpine Road. 020 7237 2376
2-5yrs. Full day

Scallywags Day Nursery
St Crispin's Church Hall,
Southwark Park Road. 020 7252 3225
2-5yrs

Trinity Childcare
Holy Trinity Church Hall, Bryan Road,
Rotherhithe. 020 7231 5842
2-5yrs. Full day

SE17
Elephant & Castle Day Nursery
15 Hampton Street. 020 7277 4488
6mths-5yrs. Full day

St Wilfrid's Montessori Pre-School
97 Lorrimore Road. 020 7701 2800
2-5yrs. Full day

SE18
Cyril Henry Nursery School
St Mary Street, Woolwich. 020 8854 0178
3-5yrs. Full day

Plumstead Manor Pre-school
020 8855 0124
3-5yrs

Visit us at
www.babydirectory.com

nurseries, private & nursery schools (cont.)

Simba Day Nursery
Artillery Place, Woolwich. 020 8317 0451
2-4yrs. Full day

Woolwich Common Nursery
Woolwich Common. 020 8854 3695
3-5yrs

SE19
Crown Point Nursery
316 Beulah Hill, Upper Norwood.
020 8766 7737
2-5yrs. Full day

Downsview Nursery
Biggin Way, Upper Norwood.
020 8764 4611
$3^1/_2$-$4^1/_2$yrs. Sessional

Little Crystal Day Nursery
49 Maberley Road, Upper Norwood.
020 8771 0393
2-5yrs. Full day

Norwood Playgroup
Crown Dale. 020 8766 6227
$2^1/_2$yrs.

Virgo Fidelis Prep
Central Hill, Upper Norwood.
020 8653 2169
$2^1/_2$-11yrs

SE20
Anerley Montessori
45 Anerley Road. 020 8778 2810
2-5yrs

Holy Trinity Playgroup
Holy Trinity Church, Lennirds Road.
020 8659 0630
3-5yrs. Mornings only

Norris Day Nursery
1 Thornsett Road, Amerley. 020 8778 9152
2-5yrs. Full day

SE21
Asquith Court Dulwich
Chancellor Grove, West Dulwich.
020 8761 6750
18mths-5yrs. Full day
See advert on page 125

Chellow Dene Day Nursery
134 Croxted Road. 020 8670 9001
18mths-5yrs. Full day

Clive Hall Day Nursery
54 Clive Road. 020 8761 9000
3mths-5yrs. Full day

Ducks in Dulwich
Dulwich College Kindergarten and Infants'
School, Eller Bank, 87 College Road.
020 8693 1538
3mths-7yrs. Full day

Dulwich College Prep
42, Alleyn Park. 020 8670 3217
$2^1/_2$-5yrs. Full day

Dulwich Montessori
St Stephen's Church, College Road.
020 8766 0091
$2^1/_2$-$5^1/_2$yrs

Little Flower Montessori
27 Turney Road. 020 8761 4178
3-5yrs. Mornings only

SE22
Bojangles Nursery School
New Life Assembly Church, Upland Road,
East Dulwich. 020 8693 2076
18mths-5yrs. Full day

Dulwich Nursery (Nursery Works)
80 Dog Kennel Hill. 020 7738 4007
3mths-5yrs. Full day
www.nurseryworks.com
See advert on page 117

First Steps Montessori Day Nursery & Pre-School
254 Uplands Road, East Dulwich.
020 8299 6897
2-5yrs. Full day

Mother Goose Nursery
248 Upland Road, East Dulwich.
020 8693 9429
1-5yrs. Full day

Oaktree Nursery
United Reform Church, Tellgrove,
East Dulwich. 020 8693 0306
$2^1/_2$-5yrs

Puddleduck Nursery
Goose Green Centre, East Dulwich Road.
020 8291 4735
$2^1/_2$-5yrs

SE23
Cottage Day Nursery
St Hilda's Church Hall, Courtrai Road.
020 8291 7117
15mths-5yrs. Full day

SE24
Halfmoon Montessori Nursery
The Methodist Church Hall,
155 Half Moon Lane. 020 7326 5300
2^1/$_2$-5yrs. Full day

Herne Hill School
Old Vicarage, 127 Herne Hill.
020 7274 6336
3-7yrs

Heron Day Nursery
St Jones Hall Lowden Road. 020 7274 2894
2-5yrs. Full day

Little Fingers Montessori Nursery
The Edward Alleyn Club, Burbage Road,
Herne Hill. 020 7274 4864
2^1/$_2$-5yrs

Ruskin House School
48 Herne Hill. 020 7737 4317
2-5yrs. Full day

SE25
Children's Paradise Day Nursery
2-4 Crowther Road, South Norwood.
020 8654 1737
3mths-5yrs. 8am-6pm

SE26
Crystal Day Nursery
202 Venner Road, Sydenham. 020 8659 6417
2-5yrs. Full day

Little Cherubs Nursery
Bell Green Lane Lower Sydenham.
020 8778 3232
3mths-5yrs. Full day

Puzzle House Nursery
Trinity Path, Sydenham. 020 8291 9844
2-5yrs

Sydenham Hill Kindergarten
Sydenham Hill Community Hall,
Sydenham Hill. 020 8693 6880
2^1/$_2$-5yrs

SE27
Noah's Ark Nursery
St Cuthberts Church, Elmcourt Road.
020 8761 1307
2-7^1/$_2$yrs

Norwood Day Nursery Co-Operative
Gypsy Road. 020 8766 6899
3mths-5yrs

One World Nursery
11 Thurlby Road. 020 8670 3511
2-4yrs. Full day

SE28
Triangle Day Nursery
61 Kellner Road, West Thamesmead
Business Park. 020 8311 4685
6wks-5yrs. Full day

SW1
**Buffer Bear at
Westminster/Bessborough Nursery**
1 Bessborough Street. 020 7641 6387
1-5yrs. Full day

Daisies Day Nursery - Pimlico
St James the Less School, Moreton Street.
020 7498 2922
From 3mths. Full day
See advert on page 132

Little House at Napier Hall
Hide Place, Vincent Square. 020 7592 0195
18mths-5yrs

Knightsbridge Kindergarten
St Peter's Church, Eaton Square.
020 7371 2306
2-5yrs

Miss Morley's Nursery School
Club Room, Fountain Court,
Buckingham Palace Road. 020 7730 5797
2^1/$_2$-5yrs

Moreton Day Nursery
Lower Ground Floor, 31 Moreton Street.
020 7233 8979. 2^1/$_2$-5yrs. Full day.
Also Moreton Day Pre-School

Moreton Day Pre-School
18 Churton Street. 020 7821 1979
6mths-5yrs

Ringrose Kindergarten Pimlico
32a Lupus Street. 020 7976 6511
2^1/$_2$-5yrs

DAISIES

DAY NURSERIES
& SCHOOLS

EXCELLENCE IN EDUCATION & DAY CARE
For children with working parents

Happy, stimulating atmosphere for babies from 3 mths to 5 year olds
Individual, loving attention & education from qualified and experienced staff
Spacious airy building with secure outside play and learning areas
Full and part time places, day care (8-6pm) with extra services for busy parents
Ofsted approved for nursery grants. Local council registered

Contact us on 020 7498 2922

Daisies Pimlico (3mths to 5 yrs)
Moreton Street, London SW1

Daisies Stockwell (2 to 5 yrs)
Jeffreys Road, London SW4

---

n

nurseries, private & nursery schools (cont.)

Thomas's Kindergarten
St Barnabas Church Hall,
14 Ranelagh Grove. 020 7730 3596
2¹/₂-4yrs

Young England Kindergarten
St Saviour's Hall, St George's Square.
020 7834 3171
2¹/₂-5yrs

SW2
Elm Park Montessori Nursery School
Brixton Hill Methodist Church, Elm Park.
020 8678 1990
2-5yrs

Little Trees Nursery
Streatham Hill & Clapham High School,
Wavertree Road. 020 8674 6912
co-ed 3-5yrs. Girls 5-18. Senior school:
Abbotswoood Road, SW16 1AW

Streatham Montessori Nursery
66 Blairderry Road. 020 8674 2208
2¹/₂-5yrs. Full day

Tiny Hands
Brockwell Park Community Centre,
Effra Parade. 020 7737 4371
2-5yrs. Full day

SW3
The Noah's Ark Nursery School/L'Arche de Noe
TAVR, Duke of York's HQ, King's Road.
020 7924 7808
3-5yrs

Ringrose Kindergarten
St Luke's Church Hall, St Luke's Street.
020 7352 8784

SW4
Abacus Pre-School Kindergarten
Clapham United Reform Church,
Grafton Square. 020 7720 7290
2-5yrs. Full day

Ark on the Park
Windmill Drive, Clapham Common.
020 8771 9014

Clapham Montessori
St Paul's Church Hall, Rectory Grove.
020 7498 8324
$2^1/2$-6yrs

Clapham Park Montessori
St James Church House, 10 West Road.
020 7498 8324
$2^1/2$-6yrs

Daisies Day School
Stockwell Methodist Church, Jeffreys Road.
020 7398 2922
$2^1/2$-5yrs. *See advert on page 132*

Elm Park Nursery
90 Clarence Avenue, Clapham.
020 8678 1990
6mths-5yrs. Full day

Eton House, The Manor Nursery School
58 Clapham Common Northside.
020 7924 6000

Magic Mind
4 Helby Road. 020 8674 5544
2-5yrs. Full day

Parkgate Montessori School
80 Clapham Common Northside.
020 7350 2452
$2^1/2$-5yrs

SW5
Ladybird Nursery School
Crypt, St Jude's Church,
24 Collingham Road. 020 7244 7771
3-5yrs. Mornings

SW6
Bumpsa Daisies
Broomhouse Lane, Fulham. 020 7736 7037
3mths-4yrs. Full day

Dawmouse Montessori Nursery
Brunswick Club, 34 Haldane Road, Fulham.
020 7381 9385
2-5$^1/2$yrs

Ivy House Nursery School
Ivy House, 233 New Kings Road.
020 7610 6900
2-5yrs. Full day

Ivy House Saplings Nursery
219 New Kings Road. 020 7610 9900
3mths-5yrs. Full day

Little People of Fulham
250A Lillie Road. 020 7386 0006
6mths-5yrs. Full day

The Little Tug Boat Day Nursery
3 Finlay Street, Fulham. 020 7731 6648
3mths-5yrs. Full day

Mucky Pups
17 Burnthwaite Road. 020 7385 6053
3mths-3yrs

Nursery on the Green
165 New Kings Road. 020 7736 6839
2-5yrs. Full day

Petits Enfants
344 Fulham Palace Road. 020 7381 2409
3mths-5yrs

Pippa Pop-ins
430 Fulham Road. 020 7385 2458

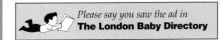

**THE CRESCENT
KINDERGARTENS**
SW17

**THE ROCKING HORSE
KINDERGARTEN**
SW6

**THE PARK
KINDERGARTEN**
SW11

A wide curriculum is taught in an exciting and stimulating way within a caring environment.

Specialist Subjects: Ballet, Music, Short Tennis & Games and French are mainly taught by specialist staff as part of the curriculum.

Spacious Facilities include a garden.

Your children will reach their potential with us academically, socially and emotionally and have a positive attitude towards learning when they join their next school.

For details please contact
Philip Evelegh
020 8772 0181

n

nurseries, private & nursery schools (cont.)

Puffins
60 Hugon Road. 020 7736 7442
0-3yrs

Rising Star Montessori School
St Clement Church Hall,
286 Fulham Palace Road. 020 7381 3511
2-5yrs

Roche Nursery School
All Saints Hall, 70 Fulham High Street.
020 8877 0823
2¹/₂-4¹/₂yrs

The Rocking Horse Kindergarten
14 Effie Road, Eelbrook Common.
020 8772 0181
2¹/₂-5yrs

Scribbles 2
St Peter's Church Hall, 2 St Peter's Terrace.
020 7381 8794
1-5yrs

Seahorses Montessori Nursery Ltd
William Thompson Memorial Hall,
Burnthwaite Road. 020 7385 7173
2¹/₂-5yrs. Full day

Seahorses Montessori Nursery II
St Etheldreda's Church Hall,
Cloncurry Street. 020 7385 7173
2-5yrs. Full day

Studio Day Nursery
93 Moore Park Road. 020 7736 9256
2-5yrs. Full day

Teddies
316 Wandsworth Bridge Road.
020 7384 3197
3mths-5yrs. Full day
www.teddiesnurseries.co.uk
See advert on page 135

Zebedee Nursery School II
Sullivan Hall, Parsons Green. 020 7371 9224
2-5yrs. Mornings

SW7
Knightsbridge Nursery School
51 Thurloe Square. 020 7584 2766
2¹/₂-5yrs

Miss Willcocks' Nursery School
Holy Trinity Church, Prince Consort Road.
020 7937 2027
$2^1/2$-5yrs

Ravenstone House
22 Queensberry Place. 020 7584 7955
2-5yrs. Full day
See advert on page 143

Pooh Corner Kindergarten
St Stephens Church Hall,
48 Emperor's Gate. 020 7373 6111
2-5yrs

Zebedee Nursery School I
St Pauls Church Hall, Onslow Square.
020 7584 7660
2-5yrs

SW8
Nine Elms Day Nursery
Savona Club House, Askalon Street.
020 7627 5191
1-5yrs. Full day

Oval Montessori Nursery
88 Fentiman Road. 020 7735 4816
3-5yrs

Springtime Day Nursery
200 Wandsworth Road. 020 7720 5255
2-5yrs. Full day

St Monica's Nursery
83-87 Clapham Road. 020 7582 0840
2-5yrs. Full day

The Willow Nursery
Clapham Baptist Church,
823-5 Wandsworth Road. 020 7498 0319
$2^1/2$-5yrs

SW9
Asquith Court Pre-School and Nursery, Lambeth
50 Groveway, Lambeth. 020 7793 9922
3mths-5yrs. Full day. *See advert on page 125*

Bunnies on the Green
United Reform Church, 60 Stockwell Road.
020 7738 4795
2-5yrs. Full day

nurseries, private & nursery schools (cont.)

Wiltshire Nursery
85 Wiltshire Road. 020 7274 4446
18mths-5yrs. Full day

SW10

Ashburnham Day Nursery
Ashburnham Community Centre,
Tetcott Road. 020 7376 5085
2-5yrs. Full day

Asquith Court Pre-School and Nursery, Battersea
18/30 Latchmere Road. 020 7228 7008.
3mths-5yrs. Full day
See advert on page 125

Blundells Traditional Teaching Nursery
The Old Court, 194-196 Sheepcote Lane.
020 7924 4204
18mths-5yrs

The Boltons Nursery School
262b Fulham Road. 020 7351 6993
2¹/2-5yrs. Full day

Bridge Lane Montessori School
23 Bridge Lane. 020 7738 0509
2¹/2-5yrs

Bumble Bee School
Church of the Ascension, Pountney Road.
020 7350 2970
2¹/2-5yrs

The Chelsea Kindergarten
St Andrew's Church, Park Walk.
020 7352 4856
2-5yrs

Clapham Junction Nursery
Asda Precinct, 204 Lavender Hill.
020 7924 1267
1-5yrs. Full day

Happy Times
40 Park Gate Road. 0800 652 2424
3mths-5yrs. Full day.
www.happytimes.co.uk.
See advert on pages 137-147

Little Red Hen
Church of the Nazarene, 2 Grant Road.
020 7738 0321
2¹/2-5yrs

Mouse House Nursery
25-27 Mallinson Road. 020 7924 1893
Co-ed 2-5yrs

Nightingale Montessori 2
Broomwood Methodist Church Hall,
Kyrle Road. 020 8675 4387
2-5yrs

Noah's Ark
St Michael's Church Hall, Cobham Close.
020 7228 9593

Paint Pots
The Chelsea Christian Centre, Edith Grove.
020 7376 4571
2¹/2-5yrs

Park Kindergarten
St Saviour's House,
351 Battersea Park Road. 020 8772 0181

Plantation Wharf Day Nursery
18 Cinammon Row, Plantation Wharf.
020 7978 5819
3mths-5yrs. Full day

Somerset Nursery School
157 Battersea Church Road. 020 7223 5455
3-5yrs

Tadpoles Nursery School
Park Walk Play Centre, Park Walk.
020 7352 9757
2¹/2-5yrs.

Thomas's Kindergarten
St Mary's Church, Battersea Church Road.
020 7738 0400
2¹/2-4yrs

Victory Day School
140 Battersea Park Road. 020 7207 1423
3mths-5yrs. Full day

Zebedee Nursery School
St Luke's Church Hall, Adrian Mews,
Ifield Road. 020 7323 5066.2-5yrs

SW12

Abacus Day Nursery
135 Laitwood Road. 020 8675 8093
18mths-5yrs. Full day

Asquith Court Nursery
36 Radbourne Road, Balham. 020 8673 1467
See advert on page 125

Caterpillar I Nursery School
74 Endlesham Road. 020 8673 6058
2¹/2-5yrs

Caterpillar II Nursery School
14a Boundaries Road. 020 8265 5224
$2^1/2$-5yrs

Gateway House Nursery School
St Jude's Church Hall, Heslop Road.
020 8675 8258. $2^1/2$-4yrs

Nightingales Nursery
St Francis Xavier College, Malwood Road.
020 8772 6056. 3mths-5yrs. Full day

Noah's Ark
Church of the Ascension, Malwood Road.
020 8772 0432

Noah's Ark Nursery School
Endlesham Church Hall,
48 Endlesham Road. 020 7228 9593

Oaktree Nursery School
21 Ramsden Road. 020 8870 8441
$2^1/2$-5yrs

Second Step Day Nursery
60 Ravenslea Road. 020 8673 6817

Wainwright Montessori School
102 Chestnut Grove. 020 8673 8037
$2^1/2$-5yrs

SW13
The Ark Nursery School
Kitson Hall, Kitson Road. 020 8741 4751
3-5yrs

Ladybird Day Nursery Montessori Nursery School
Trinity Church Road. 020 8741 1155

Montessori Pavilion
Vine Road Recreation Ground.
020 8878 9695. 3-8yrs

St Michael's Nursery School
Elmbank Gardens. 020 8567 8037
2-5yrs. Mornings

Village Nursery School
Methodist Church Hall, Station Road.
020 8878 3297. $2^1/2$-5yrs

SW14
Parkside School
459B Upper Richmond Road West.
020 8876 8144. 16mths-4yrs. Full day

Working Mums Day Care and Pre-School Centre
Mortlake Green School,
Lower Richmond Road. 020 8392 9969
3mths-5yrs

SW15
Asquith Court Putney
107-109 Norroy Road. 020 8246 5611
Full day. *See advert on page 125*

Beehive Nursery School
St Margaret's Church Hall, Putney Park
Lane. 020 8780 5333
$2^1/2$-5yrs

Bees Knees Nursery School
12 Priory Lane. 020 8876 8252. 2½-5yrs

Busy Bee Nursery
106 Felsham Road. 020 8780 1615

Busy Bee Nursery School
19 Lytton Grove. 020 8789 0132

Kingston Vale Montessori
St John's Church Lane, Robin Hood Lane,
Kingston Vale. 020 8546 3442
2-5yrs. Mornings

Noddy's Nursery School
2 Gwendolen Avenue, Putney.
020 8785 9191
4mths-5yrs. Full day

Riverside Nursery
95 Lacy Road. 020 8780 9345
3mths-5yrs. Full time

Schoolroom Montessori
St Simon's Church Hall, Hazlewell Road.
020 7384 0479. $2^1/2$-5yrs

Tiggers Nursery School
87 Putney Bridge Road. 020 8874 4668
$2^1/2$-5yrs

SW16
Abacus Early Learning Nursery
7 Drewstead Road. 020 8677 9117
18mths-5yrs. Full day

n

THE EVELINE DAY NURSERY SCHOOLS LTD

EST. 1964

Vacancies for children 3 mths to 5 years
Hours 7.30am to 6.30pm
Monday to Friday all year
(except between Christmas and New Year)

Staffed by qualified, supportive and
caring personnel in 4 Nursery branches.
With prep schools for 3-11 year olds.
The School follows the National
Curriculum with a Professional
Moderator to advise on progress.
Also educational psychologist monthly
visits are standard.

For more information and a brochure
please phone

020 8672 7549

nurseries, private & nursery schools (cont.)

Monti's Day Nursery
6 Lilian Road. 020 8876 4115
18mths-5yrs. Full day

Stepping Stones Day Nursery
496 Streatham High Road. 020 8679 4009
Part of Busy Bees

Waldorf School of South-West London
16-18 Abbotswood Road. 020 8769 6587
3^1/2-14yrs

SW17
Crescent Kindergarten I
Flat 1, 10 Trinity Crescent. 020 8772 0181

Crescent Kindergarten II
74 Trinity Road. 020 8772 0181

Eveline Day Nursery School
Seely Hall, Chillerton Road. 020 8672 0501
3mths-5yrs. Full day

Eveline Day Nursery School
30 Ritherdon Road. 020 8672 7549
3mths-5yrs. Full day

Eveline Day School
14 Trinity Crescent. 020 8672 4673
3-11yrs. Full day

Headstart
St Mary's Church Hall,
46 Wimbledon Road. 020 8947 7359
2-5yrs. Full day

Red Balloon
St Mary Magdalen Church, Trinity Road.
020 8672 4711. 2^1/2-5yrs

Teddies
Cambridge House, 272 Balham High Road.
020 8767 7109. 3mths-5yrs. Full day
www.teddiesnurseries.co.uk
See advert on page 135

Toots Day Nursery
214 Totterdown Street. 020 8767 7017
1-5yrs

SW18
Andrea's Montessori Nursery
All Saints Wandworth Parish Hall,
Lebanon Road. 020 8877 9554
2-5yrs

Eveline Day Nursery School
East Hill United Reformed Church Hall,
Geraldine Road. 020 8870 0966
3mths-5yrs. Full day

The Gardens
343 Wimbledon Park Road. 020 8947 7058
2^1/2-5yrs

Jigsaw Early Years
Dolphin House, Riverside West,
Smugglers Way, Wandsworth.
020 8877 1135
www.jigsawgroup.com

Melrose House Nursery School
39 Melrose Road. 020 8874 7769
2^1/2-5yrs

Noah's Ark
Westside Church Hall, Melody Road.
020 7228 9593. 2^1/2-5yrs

Roche School
11 Frogmore. 020 8877 0823. 3-11yrs

Schoolroom Two
Southfields Lawn Tennis Club,
Gressenhall Road, Southfields.
020 8874 9305. 2^1/2-5yrs

nurseries, private & nursery schools (cont.)

Schoolroom Two
Southfields Lawn Tennis Club,
Gressenhall Road, Southfields.
020 8874 9305. 2^1/$_2$-5yrs

Sticky Fingers Montessori Day Nursery
St John the Divine Church Hall,
Garratt Lane, Wandsworth. 020 8871 9496
18mths-5yrs. Full day

Teddies
Duntshill Mill, 21 Riverdale Drive.
020 8870 2009
3mths-5yrs. Full day
www.teddiesnurseries.co.uk
See advert on page 135

Three-Four-Five
Fitzhugh Community Hall, Trinity Road.
020 8870 8441

Wandle House Nursery School
25 West Hill. 020 8875 0752
2-5yrs

Wee Ones Nursery School
St Anne's Church Hall, St Ann's Hill,
Wandsworth. 020 8870 7729
2^1/$_2$-5yrs

Wimbledon Park Montessori Nursery School
206 Heythorp Street. 020 8944 8584
2^1/$_2$-5yrs

SW19
Buffer Bear Nursery
Wimbledon Traincare Depot,
Durnsford Road. 020 944 5618
3mths-5yrs. Full day

Castle Kindergarten
20 Henfield Road. 020 8544 0089

Cosmopolitan Day Nursery
65-67 High Street, Colliers Wood.
020 8544 0758
2^1/$_2$yrs. Full day

Crown Kindergarten
Coronation House, Ashcombe Road.
020 8540 8820
2-5yrs

Eveline Day Nursery School
89a Quicks Road. 020 8545 0699
3mths-5yrs. Full day
See advert on page 138

Herbert Day Nursery
52a Dundonald Road. 020 8542 7416
Full day

The Hill Kindergarten
65 Wimbledon Hill Road. 020 8946 7467
2^1/$_2$-3yrs.

Little Hall Gardens
49 Durnsford Avenue. 020 8947 7058
1-5yrs. Full day

Maria Montessori Nursery
St John's Ambulance Hall,
122-124 Kingston Road. 020 8543 6353
2-5yrs. Mornings

Noddy's Nursery School
Trinity Church Hall, Beaumont Road,
West Hill. 020 8785 9191

Nutkins Nursery
Beaumont Road. 020 8246 6400
2-5yrs. Full day

Playdays
58 Queens Road. 020 8946 8139
3mths-5yrs. Full day. Training college
See advert on page 148

St Mark's Montessori
St Mark's Church, St Mark's Place.
0956 346938
2^1/$_2$-5yrs. Mornings

Sunny-side Nursery School
ATC Hall, 192 Merton Road, South
Wimbledon. 020 8337 0887
2^1/$_2$-5yrs. Mornings

Trinity Nursery School
Holy Trinity Church Centre. 020 8540 3868
2^1/$_2$-5yrs. Full day

Wimbledon Jewish Nursery
1 Queensmere Road. 020 8946 4836

SW20
Coombe Montessori Nursery
Wimbledon College Playing Fields,
183 Coombe Lane. 020 8946 3822
2^1/$_2$-5yrs. Full day

Raynes Park Nursery
c/o David Lloyd Leisure Club, Bushey
Road, Raynes Park. 020 8543 9005
Part of Busy Bees

Ursuline Convent Prep
18 The Downs. 020 8947 0859
Boys 3-7yrs/Girls 3-11yrs

SW29
Dees Day Nursery
2 Mansel Road. 020 8944 0284
3mths-5yrs. Full day

*Full listings for TW nurseries can be
found in the Local Baby Directory:
Surrey & S. Middlesex*

TW1
Teddies
3 March Road. 020 8744 9643
3mths-5yrs. Full day
www.teddiesnurseries.co.uk
See advert on page 135

TW8
Grove Terrace Park
020 8400 9648
18mths-5yrs. Full day

**Brentford Day Nursery (Bringing up
Baby)**
Half Acre, Brentford. 020 8568 7561
3mths-5yrs. Full day
www.bringingupbaby.co.uk
See advert on page 123

Teddies
Old School Building, The Ham.
020 8847 3799
3mths-5yrs. Full day
www.teddiesnurseries.co.uk
See advert on page 135

W1
Great Beginnings Montessori School
82a Chiltern Street. 020 7486 2276. 2-6yrs

Jumbo Nursery School
St James's Church Hall, 22 George Street.
020 7935 2441. 2-5yrs. Mornings

Marylebone Kindergarten
34/36 Crawford Street. 020 7224 9653
www.kids.uk.com
3mths-5yrs. Full day
See advert on page 142

W2
**Buffer Bear at Westminster/Warwick
Nursery**
Cirencester Street. 020 7641 4361
1-5yrs. Full day

Dr Rolfe's Montessori School
10 Pembridge Square. 020 7727 8300
$2^1/2$-5yrs

**Kinderland Montessori Nursery
School**
47 Palace Court. 020 7792 1964
2-5yrs

Paintpots Montessori School
Bayswater United Reform Church.
12 Newton Road. 020 7792 0433
$2^1/2$-5yrs. Full day

Ravenstone House
Long Gardens, Albion Street. 020 7262 1190
www.ravenstonehouse.co.uk
$2^1/2$mths-7yrs. Full day
See advert on page 143

St John's Montessori Nursery School
St John's Church Hall,
Hyde Park Crescent. 020 7402 2529
2-5yrs

W3
Bizzy Lizzy Day Nursery
c/o The Priory Community Centre,
Acton Lane. 020 8993 1664
2-5yrs. Full day

Buffer Bear Nursery
10 Stanley Gardens. 020 8743 7249
3mths-5yrs. Full day

n

nurseries, private & nursery schools (cont.)

Buttercups Day Nursery
27 Old Oak Road. 020 8740 7109
3mths-4$^{1}/_{2}$yrs. Full day

Carousel Nursery
Acton Hill Church Centre,
Woodlands Avenue. 020 8896 3663
2-5yrs. Full day

Cybertots
1 Avenue Crescent. 020 8752 0200
2-5yrs. Full day

Ealing Montessori School
St Martin's Church Hall,
5 Hale Gardens. 020 8992 4513
2$^{1}/_{2}$-5yrs

Happy Child Day Nursery
St Gabriel's Church, Noel Road.
020 8992 0855
6mths-5yrs. Full day
www.happychild.co.uk
See advert on page 119

Village Montessori School
All Saints Church Centre,
Bollo Bridge Road. 020 8993 3540. 2$^{1}/_{2}$-5yrs

W4
Buttercups Day Nursery
38 Grange Road. 020 8995 6750
3mths-5yrs. Full day

Caterpillar Montessori Nursery
St Albans Church Hall, South Parade.
020 8747 8531
2$^{1}/_{2}$-5yrs

n

nurseries, private & nursery schools (cont.)

Chiswick Community Nursery
53 Barrowgate Road. 020 8995 2180
6mths-5yrs. Full day

Chiswick Toddlers World
St Paul's Church Hall, Pyrmont Road.
020 8995 7267. 1-5yrs. Full day

Corner House Day Nursery
Heathfield Gardens. 020 8995 7585
3mths-5yrs. Full day

Elmwood Montessori
St Michaels Centre, Elmwood Road.
020 8994 8177

Imaginations
Methodist Church Hall, Sutton Court Road.
020 8994 5422. 2-5yrs

Meadows Montessori
Dukes Meadow Community Hall,
Alexandra Gardens. 020 8742 1327

Our Lady Queen of Peace Day Nursery
10 Chiswick Lane. 020 8994 2053
2-5yrs

Parkside Nursery School
Homefield Lodge, Chiswick Lane North.
020 8995 4648
2-6yrs. Mornings only

Riverside Children's Centre
Cavendish School, Edensor Road.
020 8995 9299
2-5yrs. Full day

Riverside Teddies Day Nursery
Riverside Club, Dukes Meadow.
020 8987 1831. 3mths-5yrs. Full day
www.teddiesnurseries.co.uk
See advert on page 135

Tara House
Scout Haven Wilson Walk. 020 8995 5144
2-5yrs

Teddies
The Old Chapel, Evershed Walk (formerly
Acton Lane). 020 8995 4766
3mths-5yrs. Full day
www.teddiesnurseries.co.uk
See advert on page 135

Westside Day Nursery
Steele Road. 020 8742 2206
3mths-$2^1/2$yrs yrs. Full day

W5
Buttercups Day Nursery
9 Florence Road. 020 8840 4838
3mths-5yrs

Caterpillar Day Nursery
8th Ealing Scout Hall, Popes Lane.
020 8579 0833. 2-5yrs. Full day

Children's Garden
35 Gunnersbury Avenue. 020 8896 0450
Steiner

Happy Child Day Nursery
283-287 Windmill Road. 020 8567 2244
3mths-5yrs. Full day
www.happychild.co.uk
See advert on page 119

Happy Child Day Nursery
Woodgrange Avenue. 020 8992 0209
3mths-5yrs. Full day
www.happychild.co.uk
See advert on page 119

Happy Child Day Nursery
2b The Grove. 020 8567 4300
3mths-5yrs. Full day
www.happychild.co.uk
See advert on page 119

Happy Child Day Nursery
2a The Grove. 020 8566 1546
1-5yrs. Full time. www.happychild.co.uk
See advert on page 119

Happy Child Montessori School
Welsh Chapel, Ealing Green. 020 8840 9936
2-5yrs. Full day. *See advert on page 119*

Jumpers Nursery
YMCA, 25 St Mary's Road. 020 8799 4871
$2^1/2$-5yrs

Nursery Land Daycare Centre
9th Ealing Scouts Hut, Northfield Avenue.
020 8566 5962. 2-4yrs

Mount Park Montessori School
St Andrew's Church, Mount Park Road.
020 8560 8174. $2^1/2$-5yrs

New World Montessori Nursery School
St Barnabus Millenium Church Hall,
Pitshanger Lane. 020 8810 4411
2-5yrs

Resurrection Day Nursery
84 Gordon Road. 020 8998 8954
2-5yrs

St Matthew's Montessori School
St Matthew's Church Hall,
North Common Road. 020 8579 2304
2-5yrs

Tortoise Green Nursery School
43 Castlebar Road. 020 8998 0638. 3-5yrs

W6
Bayonne Nursery School
50 Paynes Walk. 020 7385 5366. 3-5yrs

The Beanstalk Montessori Nursery School
St Peter's Church, Black Lion Lane.
020 8740 7891. 2¹/₂-5yrs

Butterflies & Bumblebees
20 Nigel Playfair Avenue. 010 7734 9501
Steiner

Flora Nursery
Community Centre, Flora Gardens.
020 8748 0750. 2¹/₂-5yrs. Full day

Happy Times
The Stamford (ex Royal Masonic Hospital),
Ravenscourt Park. www.happytimes.co.uk
0800 652 2424. 3mths-5yrs. 7am-7pm
See advert on pages 137-147

Howard House Nursery School
58 Ravenscourt Road, Ravenscourt Park.
020 8741 5147. 2¹/₂-5yrs. Mornings

Jigsaw Day Nursery
Centre West, Hammersmith Broadway.
020 8563 7982. www.jigsawgroup.com
3mths-5yrs. Full day. *See advert on page 139*

Jordans Nursery School
Lower Hall, Holy Innocents Church,
Paddenswick Road. 020 8741 3230

**Richford Street Day Nursery
(Bringing Up Baby)**
50 Richford Gate, 61-69 Richford Street.
020 8746 1015. 3mths-5yrs. Full day
www.bringingupbaby.co.uk
See advert on page 123

Rose Montessori School
St Albans Church Hall, Margravine Road.
020 7381 6002
2¹/₂-5yrs

W7
Bunny Park Day Nursery
37 Manor Court Road. 020 8567 6142
2-4yrs. Full day

Buttons Nursery School
99 Oaklands Road. 020 8840 3355
2¹/₂-5yrs

Fairytale Day Nursery
Leighton Hall, Elthorne Park Road.
020 8840 2851
2-5yrs. Full day

Sticky Fingers Day Nursery
Bernard Sunley Hall, Greenford Avenue.
020 8566 4606
2-5yrs. Full day

W8
The Playroom
Etheline Hall, Denbigh Road.
020 7376 1804
2-5yrs

Iverna Gardens Montessori Nursery School
Armenian Church Hall, Iverna Gardens.
www.iverna.com. 020 7937 0794
2¹/₂-5yrs

nurseries, private & nursery schools (cont.)

W9

Buffer Bear at Westminster/St Jude's
88 Bravington Road. 020 7641 5837
1-5yrs. Full day

Buffer Bear at Westminster/St Stephens Nursery
The Annexe, Essendine Road. 020 7641 4346
6mths-5yrs. Full day

Little Sweethearts Montessori School
St Saviour's Church Hall, Warwick Avenue.
020 7266 1616. 2-7yrs

Windmill Montessori Nursery School
Former Caretaker's Cottage,
Oakington Road. 020 7289 3410. 2-5yrs

W10

Buffer Bear at Westminster/Katharine Bruce Nursery
Queens Park Court, Ilbert Street.
020 7641 5835. 1-5yrs. Full day

Garden House Nursery School
210 Latimer Road. 020 8968 2922
2-5yrs

Sunrise Pre-School
Moberly Sports Centre, Kilburn Lane.
020 8968 2921
2-5yrs

Tiny Tots Nursery
St Quintin Health Centre,
St Quintin Avenue. 020 8960 2020
3mths-4yrs

W11

Cherry Tree Pre-Nursery School
St Francis of Assisi Community Centre,
Pottery Lane. 020 8961 2081
18mths-3^1/₂yrs

Complete Nursery
11 Pembridge Mews. 020 7727 8590
2-5yrs

Gate Nursery School
Garden flat, 77 Clarendon Road.
020 7221 2094
2-4yrs

Holland Park Nursery School
The Undercroft, St John's Church,
Lansdowne Crescent. 020 7221 2194
2^1/₂-5yrs

Ladbroke Square Montessori School
43 Ladbroke Square. 020 7229 0125
2^1/₂-5yrs

Maria Montessori Children's House Notting Hill
All Saints Church, 28 Powis Gardens.
www.montessori-ami.org. 020 7221 4141
2^1/₂-5yrs

Miss Delaney's Nursery
St James, Norland Church, St James's
Gardens. 020 7603 6095. 2^1/₂-5yrs

Miss Delaney's Too
St Clement's Church, 95 Sirdar Road.
020 7727 0010. 2^1/₂-5yrs

The Mynors' Nursery School
Garden flat, 4 Chepstow Villas.
020 7727 7253. 2^1/₂-5yrs

St Peters Nursery School
59a Portobello Road. 020 7243 2617
2^1/₂-5yrs

The Square Montessori School
18 Holland Park Avenue. 020 7221 6004
2^1/₂-5yrs

Strawberry Fields Nursery School
5 Pembridge Villas. 020 7727 8363
2^1/₂-5yrs

Toddlers Inn Montessori
The Rugby Club, 223 Walmer Road.
020 7727 6309. 2-5yrs

Villas Nursery School
32 St Ann's Villas, Holland Park Avenue.
020 7602 6232
2-5yrs. Full day

W12

Ladybird Day Nursery
Sulgrave Club, 287 Goldhawk Road.
020 8846 8519
6mths-5yrs. Full day

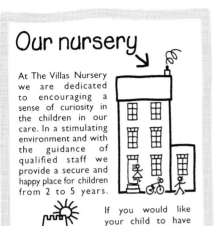

Our nursery

At The Villas Nursery we are dedicated to encouraging a sense of curiosity in the children in our care. In a stimulating environment and with the guidance of qualified staff we provide a secure and happy place for children from 2 to 5 years.

The Villas Nursery
32 St.Ann's Villas
Holland Park
W11 4RS

If you would like your child to have the best possible start, call us now for our brochure about full day care and term time classes.

Tel: 020 7602 6232
www.daycare.co.uk

Ladybird Montessori
277 Goldhawk Road. 020 8741 3399
2-5yrs

Little People of Shepherds Bush
61 Hadyn Park Road. 020 8749 5080
6mths-3yrs *See advert on page 133*

Little People of Willow Vale
9 Willow Vale. 020 8749 2877. 3-5yrs

Shepherds Bush Day Nursery (Bringing Up Baby)
101 Frithville Gardens. 020 8749 1256
3mths-5yrs. Full day
www.bringingupbaby.co.uk
See advert on page 123

Vanessa Nursery School
14 Cathnor Road. 020 8743 8196
3-5yrs

W13
Children's Corner
29 Hastings Road. 020 8840 5591
18mths-5yrs. Full day

Corner House Day Nursery
82 Lavington Road. 020 8567 2806
3mths-5yrs. Full day

Happy Child Baby Nursery
Green Man Passage (off Bayham Road).
020 8566 5515. 3mths-2^1/$_2$yrs
www.happychild.co.uk
See advert on page 119

Monks Nursery
5 Monks Drive. 020 8992 5104
18mths-3yrs

Jigsaw
1 Courtfield Gardens. 020 8997 8330
18mths-5yrs. Full day
See advert on page 139

Playways Early Learning School
2 Amhert Road. 020 8998 2723
3mths-5yrs. Full day

West London YMCA Noah's Ark Nursery
2a Drayton Green. 020 8810 6769
2-5yrs

W14
Bright Sparks Montessori School
25 Minford Gardens. 020 7371 4697
2^1/$_2$-5yrs

Busy Bee Nursery
Addison Boys Club, Redan Street.
020 7602 8905. 3-5yrs

Holland Park Day Nursery
9 Holland Road. 020 7602 9066
3mths-2yrs. Full day

n **nurseries, private & nursery schools (cont.)**

Little Lillies
76-80 Lillie Road. 020 7381 0670
$2^1/2$-5yrs. Mornings

Playdays
13 Barton Road. 020 7386 9083
3mths-5yrs. Full day

Playdays
45 Comeragh Road. 020 7385 1955
3mths-5yrs. Full day

Ripples Montessori School
The Crypt, St John the Baptist Church,
Holland Road. 020 7602 7433
$2^1/2$-5yrs.

School House
5 Holland Road. 020 7602 9066
2-8yrs. Full day

Sinclair Montessori Nursery School
Garden flat, 142 Sinclair Road.
020 7602 3745. $2^1/2$-$5^1/2$yrs

WC1
Coram Fields Nursery
93 Guildford Street. 020 7833 0198
3-5yrs

Kids Unlimited@Mango Tree
Amnesty International, 25 Easton Street.
020 7278 2214
From 3mths-4yrs. Full day

Thomas Coram Early Childhood Centre
49 Mecklenburgh Square. 020 7520 0385
6mths-5yrs

WC2
Chandos Day Nursery
47 Dudley Court, 36 Endell Street.
020 7836 6574
3mths-5yrs. Full day

Fleet Street Nursery
4 Wild Court. 020 7831 9179
From 3mths. Full day

Kingsway Children's Centre
4 Wild Court. 020 7831 7460
From 3mths. Full day

Babylist

The advisory and supply service

Let Babylist take the strain.
Within *Babylist's* comfortable London showroom view the
latest Nursery furniture and equipment. Beautiful baby
and maternity clothing. Birth and christening stationery
to order. Sit back and relax while our experienced
consultants give you
independent advice
tailored to your own
personal needs.

Our extensive range,
includes Simon Horn
(Cot/bed/sofa), Bill
Amberg (sling), Euro
Baby, Petit Bateau, Dior, and *Babylist's* own exclusive
furniture range. And don't worry
about heavy packages - we deliver
straight to your door!
"*Babylist - the ultimate advisory and
supply service for pregnant mums*".
Nicola Fornby, Telegraph.

Tel: 020 7371 5145   Fax: 020 7371 5245
email: info@babylist.co.uk   www: babylist.co.uk

nursery advisory service

Baby List Company
The Broomhouse, 50 Sulivan Road, SW6.
020 7371 5145
www.babylist.co.uk
See advert on page 149

n

nursery furniture & decor

(see also mail order: nursery furniture, murals and painted furniture, nursery goods)

Feng Shui Partnership
020 8883 1261

Jafino
Freepost, Jafino. 01706 870602

Tots to Teens
01438 815355

Willey Winkle
Offa House, Offa Street, Hereford.
01432 268018
Traditional mattresses

ELJ Design
0958 646 113
Decorative painter, specialising in
nurseries. *See advert under murals*

Ben's Beds
07930 406610

NW2
Ikea
Brent Park. 020 8208 5600

NW8
Mark Wilkinson
41 St John's Wood High Street.
020 7586 9579

SW3
Dragons of Walton Street
23 Walton Street. 020 7589 3795
Hand-painted children's furniture

nursery furniture & decor (cont.)

Nursery Window
83 Walton Street. 020 7581 3358

Holding Company
241-245 Kings Road. 020 7352 1600
Good storage ideas

SW4
Cheeky Monkey
24 Abbeville Road. 020 8673 5215
See advert under toy shops

SW6
Simon Horn
117-121 Wandsworth Bridge Road.
020 7731 1279
See advert on page 151

Blue Lemon
160 Munster Road. 020 7610 9464

SW11
Little Bridge
56 Battersea Bridge Road. 020 7978 5522

SW13
Tobias and the Angel
66 White Hart Lane. 020 8296 0058

SW15
Putney Painted Pieces
20 Lower Richmond Road. 020 8788 0830

W4
Red Studio
12a Spring Grove. 020 8994 7770

W6
The Back Store
330 King Street. 020 8741 5022

W11
Mark Wilkinson
126 Holland Park. 020 7727 5814

WC2
The Children's Seating Centre
11 Whitcomb Street (off Trafalgar Square).
020 7930 8308

nursery goods

(see also clothing shops, mail order)

Check out the new Baby Directory Shop on www.babydirectory.com for a comprehensive and competitively priced selection of nursery goods.

E2
Potty People
31-318 Bethnal Green Road. 020 7729 2217

Khalsa
388 and 418 Bethnal Green Road.
020 7729 3286

E5
Kiddi Centre
147 Clapton Common. 020 8809 4251

E8
E.Gibbons
7-17 Amhurst Road. 020 8985 3129

Family Care
90-94 Kingsland High Street. 020 7254 8720

E17
Victoria 2 Nursery Goods
246 Hoe Street. 020 8521 2798

Baby This 'N' Baby That
359 Forest Road. 020 8527 4002

N1
Baby Munchkins
186 Hoxton Street. 020 7684 5994

N8
Gooseberry Bush
15 Park Road. 020 8342 9898
See advert under maternity wear

N12
All Seasons Nursery Shop
654-656 High Road, Tally Ho Corner.
020 8445 6314

N22
London Nursery Supplies
Hardy Passage, Berners Road.
020 8889 3003

The Nearly New
Childrenswear & Nursery Store
131 Walham Green Court
Moore Park Road, SW6 2DG

Tel/Fax: 020 7381 6464
e-mail: halshouse@hotmail.com

SE6
Swaddling & Co
21-23 Rushey Green. 020 8697 2992

SE22
C & G Baby Shop
15-17 Lordship Lane. 020 8693 4504

SW3
Conran Shop
81 Fulham Road. 020 7589 7401

SW6
Baby List Company
The Broomhouse, 50 Sulivan Road.
020 7371 5145
See advert on page 149

Baby World
239 Munster Road. 020 7386 1904

Hal's House
131 Walham Green Court, Moore Park
Road. 020 7381 6464
halshouse@hotmail.com

SW8
Lilliput
255/259 Queenstown Road. 020 7720 5554

SW12
Babies Product Centre
76 Balham High Road. 020 8333 9067

Bebeworld
191 Balham High Road. 020 8675 8871
Also pram repairs

n

ZITA WEST

*straightforward help and
reassurance for modern couples.*

A superb range of natural fertility
& pregnancy products specially
formulated by a Harley St
practitioner and acupuncturist

www.zitawest.com
Tel 0870 166 8899

nursery goods (cont.)

SW15
Lilliput
278 Upper Richmond Road. 020 8780 1682

SW19
Lilliput
100 Haydons Road. 020 8542 3542

W4
Pixies
14 Fauconberg Road. 020 8995 1568
See advert under nearly new

W13
Daniel Nursery Centre
96-122 Uxbridge Road. 020 8567 6789

■ *Kent*
The Wendy House
20 The Broadway, High Street, Sheerness.
01795 666625

nursery teacher recruitment

**Montessori Teachers & Nannies
Employment Agency**
107 Bow Road, Bow, E3. 020 8981 8118
See advert under nanny agencies

nutrition

British Dietetic Association
0121 616 4900

Foresight
01483 427839

**Wellbeing Eating for Pregnancy
Helpline**
0114 242 4084

www.zitawest.com
0870 166 8899

The Centre for Nutritional Medicine
114 Harley Street, W1. 020 7224 5053

one o'clock clubs

A wonderful invention! Open usually Monday-Friday, 1-4pm, maybe longer on holidays, one o'clock clubs provide painting equipment, trikes, water play, balls, etc, in addition to basic playground equipment. There is usually an indoor and an outdoor section. They are generally free, and open to under 5s.

N1
Barnard Park
Copenhagen Street. 020 7278 9494

St Paul's
The Playbuildings, St Paul's Open Space, Marquess Estate

N4
Jamboree One O'Clock Club
The Playhuts, Seven Sisters Gate, Finsbury Park. 020 8802 1301
10am-3pm. Tues, Wed, Thurs

N5
The Bandstand
Highbury Fields.
020 7704 9337

N19
Whittington Park Building
Yerbury Road. 020 7263 6896

N22
The Grove
Alexandra Park

NW3
Parliament Hill
Highgate Road

NW5
Peggy Jay Centre
Parliament Hill Fields. 020 7485 6907

NW10
Queens Park

SE1
Geraldine Harnsworth Park
St George's Road. 020 7820 9724

SE5
John Ruskin One O'Clock Club
John Ruskin Park, Denmark Hill, Camberwell. 020 7733 6659 Closed Friday

Kennington Park
Bolton Crescent, off Camberwell Road.
020 7735 7186

Myatts Fields
Cormont Road. 020 7733 3609
Closed Wednesday

SE15
Leyton One O'Clock Playroom
Leyton Square, Peckham Park Road.
020 7639 1812

Peckham One O'Clock Playroom
Peckham Rye Road (opposite Barry Road).
020 8693 0481

SE16
Southwark One O'Clock Playroom
Southwark Park, Hawkstone Road.
020 7231 3755

SE26
Crystal Palace

SE27
Norwood Park
Salters Hill. Closed Tuesday

SW2
Hillside Gardens
Hillside Road. 020 8678 0698

Windmill Gardens
Blenheim Gardens (behind Brixton prison).
020 8671 5587. Closed Tuesday

SW4
Clapham Common
Windmill Drive. 020 8673 5736
Closed Friday

Agnes Riley Gardens
Corner Clarence Avenue/Poynders Road.
020 8673 1277. Closed Thursday

 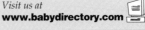

one o'clock clubs (cont.)

W6
Bishops Park
Stevenage Road

SW8
John Milton
194 Thessaly Road, Battersea Park Road

Larkhall Park
Priory Court, off Lansdowne Way.
020 7627 0009. Closed Monday

Vauxhall Park
Fentiman Road. Closed Tuesday

SW9
Brockwell Park
Arlingford Road. 020 8671 4883
Closed Wednesday

Heathbrook Park
St Rule Street

Loughborough Park Play Project
Moorland Road. 020 7926 1049
Closed Thursday

Max Roach Park
Wiltshire Road, Community Centre.
020 7274 6693. Closed Monday

Slade Gardens
Robsart Street. 020 7733 3630
Closed Thursday

SW11
Battersea Park
Prince of Wales Drive

York Gardens Community Centre
Lavender Road. 020 8871 8821

SW12
Triangle
Tooting Bec Common, off Emmanuel Road

SW16
Streatham Vale Park
Abercairn Road. 020 8764 3688
Closed Monday

SW18
Bolingbroke Grove
Chivalry Road, Wandsworth Common

King George's Park
Buckhold Road

The Windmill
Windmill Road/Heathfield Road

SW19
Colliers Wood One O'Clock Club
Colliers Wood Pavilion, Clarendon Road

TW1
Marble Hill Park
Marble Hill Park, Richmond Road,
Twickenham. 020 8891 0641
Small charge

W2
One O'Clock Club
Paddington Rec

W3
Acton Park Playcentre
East Acton Lane. 020 8743 6133
Closed Mons, weekend afternoons

W4
Rainbow Play House
Recreation Playground, Homefields,
Chiswick Lane. 020 8995 4648

W6
Under Fives Centre
Ravenscourt Park. 020 8748 3180

W9
Paddington Rec
Randolph Avenue

W10
Kensington Memorial Park
St Marks Road

Little Wormwood Scrubs
Dalgarno Gardens

Meanwhile Gardens
Elkstone Road

W12
Cathnor Playhouse
Cathnor Road. 020 8743 7271

Under Fives
New Zealand Way, White City Estate.
020 8743 9958

W13
Llamas Park Playcentre
Elers Road. 020 8810 0240

Pitshanger Park Playcentre
Meadowvale Road. 020 8998 1918

W14
Holland Park
Abbotsbury Road

organic

Babynat
020 8340 0401
www.organico.co.uk
See advert under food

Beaming Baby
0800 0345 672
www.beamingbaby.com
See advert under nappies

Green Baby
345 Upper Street, London N1. 020 7226 4345
www.greenbabyco.com

KPC (Kensington Provision Company)
020 7386 7778

Little Green Earthlets
163 Lower Richmond Road, SW15.
020 8780 3075
mail order: 01825 873301
www.earthlets.co.uk
See advert under nappies, cloth & other

Organic Baby Co
01323 411515
www.theorganicbabyco.com

Organic Delivery Co.
020 7739 8181

Planet Organic
42 Westbourne Grove, W2. 020 7221 7171

Simply Organic Food Ltd
020 7622 5006
www.simplyorganic.net

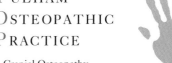

FULHAM
OSTEOPATHIC
PRACTICE

• Cranial Osteopathy
• Gentle treatment for mother and baby
• Easy access and parking

☎ 020 7384 1851

osteopaths

(see also craniosacral therapy)

General Osteopathic Council
Osteopathy House, 176 Tower Bridge Road,
London SE1. 020 7357 6655

N8
Crouch End Natural Health Clinic
170 Weston Park. 020 8341 9800

NW3
British College of Naturopathy and Osteopathy
6 Netherhall Gardens, Hampstead.
020 7435 7830

NW5
The College Practice
60 Highgate Road. 020 7267 6445

SW6
Fulham Osteopathic Practice
53 Finlay Street. 020 7384 1851
Child-friendly, easy parking, ground floor

SW11
The Battersea Osteopathic Practices
2B Ashness Road, Webb's Road entrance.
020 7738 9199
Also Cranial Osteopathy Clinic

SW19
Nik Casse
Albany Clinic, 277 The Broadway, 1st floor,
Wimbledon. 020 8542 4455

Krystyna Zielinski
18 Daybrook Road. 020 8542 8596

W1
Osteopathic Centre for Children
109 Harley Street. 020 7486 6160

The Hale Clinic
7 Park Crescent. 020 7631 0156. Also cranial

W3
Susan Farwell, Sarah Towers, Matthew Stones
1st floor, Capital House, 11 Market Place.
020 8993 1994

W4
R. Adegoke
17 Thorney Hedge Road. 020 8987 8581

W12
West London Osteopaths
65 Vespan Road. 020 8749 0581

outings

(see also farms, indoor adventure playcentres, museums, parks, theatres, zoos)

Always ring to check opening times and avoid disappointment. If you are travelling outside the area covered by this book, don't forget to arm yourself with the necessary *Local Baby Directory*. We now cover:

- Bristol & Bath
- Herts & Middlesex
- Oxfordshire, Berks & Bucks
- South Wales
- Sussex & Hampshire
- Surrey S. Middlesex

■ *Information lines*

London Tourist Board What's On for Children Line
0839 123 404

London Tourist Information Service
Children's London. 0839 337799

■ *In town*

EC1
Imax Cinema
Roundabout, Waterloo Station.
020 7902 1234
UK's biggest screen

EC3
Tower of London
Tower Hill. 020 7709 0765
Crown Jewels, Armoury.
Mon-Sat 9-6pm, winter 9.30-5pm. Sun 10-6pm, winter 10-5pm. Tube to Tower Hill

NW1
London Planetarium
Marylebone Road. 020 7935 6861

Madame Tussaud's
Baker Street.
Too frightening for tinies. And the queue…
Tube to Baker Street

SE1
HMS Belfast
Morgan's Lane, off Tooley Street.
020 7940 6300

London Aquarium
County Hall, Westminster Bridge Road.
020 7967 8000

London Eye
0870 5000 600
Bit dull for tinies

London Frog Tours
County Hall, Riverside Buildings, Westminster Bridge Road. 020 7928 3132
Amphibious craft, river and road tour

SW1
Changing the Guard
Buckingham Palace, The Mall.
Daily 11.30am from April to end of July.
Alternate days in winter.

Royal Mews
Buckingham Palace. 020 7930 4832

WC2
Cabaret Mechanical Theatre
33-34 The Market, Covent Garden.
020 7739 7961
Intricate automata worked by pushing buttons or turning levers

■ *Out of town*

■ *Berkshire*
Legoland
Winkfield Road, Windsor. 0990 040 404
Jct 6 off M4, Jct 3 off M3. Train from Waterloo + shuttle bus

Look Out Discovery Park
Nine Mile Road, Bracknell. 01344 868 222
Environmental family park. Combine with Coral Reef. M4, Jct 10, A322 signs for Bagshot

Windsor Castle
Windsor. 01753 868286

■ *Buckinghamshire*
Bekonscot Model Village
Warwick Road, Beaconsfield. 01494 672919

Marlow Park
Marlow.
M40, off at Jct 4, towards Marlow. Great
playground

■ *Hertfordshire*
Chiltern Open Air Museum
Newlands Park, Calfton Lane, Gorelands.
01494 871117
Closed in winter

■ *Middlesex*
Heathrow Airport Visitor Centre
Newell Road, off the Northern Perimeter,
Heathrow Airport. 020 8745 6655

The London Butterfly House
Syon Park, Brentford. 020 8560 7272
Tropical butterflies, toads, iguanas.
Aquarium. Can be combined with Snakes
and Ladders indoor adventure playground
and the garden centre

■ *Kent*
Leeds Castle
Maidstone. 01622 765400

■ *Surrey*
Chessington World of Adventures
Leatherhead Road, Chessington.
01372 729 560
Theme park and zoo. Jct 9 off M25 or A3

Hampton Court Palace
East Molesey. 020 8781 9500
Children's trail and maze. M25 Jct 10, A307
or Jct 12, A308.

Thorpe Park
Staines Road, Chertsey. 01932 569393
White knuckle water rides

paddling pools

*(see parks & playground section for details, see
also swimming pools: outdoor)*

☺ = recommended

E9 ....Victoria Park
N8 .... Priory Park
N16 .... Clissold Park
N22 .... Alexandra Palace Park
NW5 .... Parliament Hill
NW10 .... ☺ Queen's Park
SE5 .... Burgess Park
.... Ruskin Park
SW1................................. Causton Street
SW4 .... Clapham Common
SW6 .... ☺ Bishop's Park
SW10 .... Cremorne Gardens
SW13 .... Castelnau Recreation Ground
         Washington Road/Barnes Avenue
         .... Palewell Common
                                             East Sheen
         ....Vine Road Recreation Ground
                                      Vine Road, Barnes
SW18 .... Streatham Common
SW19................................ Dundonald Park
                                      Wimbledon Park
Kew ...... North Sheen Recreation Ground
W1 .... Hyde Park
W6 .... ☺ Ravenscourt Park
W10 .... Meanwhile Gardens
W11 .... Memorial Park
                                             St Mark's Road
W13 .... Cranleigh Gardens
WC1 .... Coram's Fields
W12 .... Hammersmith Park

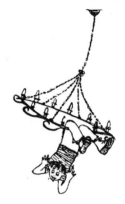

Reproduced by kind permission of **The Dodo Pad**©
"The perfect antidote to organisational chaos".
See advertisement under gifts

parent & toddler groups

(see also mother & baby groups, playgroups)

These are mainly for parents or carers with children under 3 years, but some extend to under 5s. Usually run by parents, they are held in church halls, etc, and carers remain with the children. There is usually a small charge. Ring your local council *(see councils)* for venues near you, or check notice boards in clinics, hospitals and libraries.

parentcraft classes & advice

Crêchendo Training
1 Grange Mills, Weir Road, SW12.
020 8772 8160
training@crechendo.com
www.crechendo.com
See advert under first aid

The Parent Company
6 Jacob's Wells Mews, W1. 020 7935 0123
www.theparentcompany.co.uk

Babycare
020 7386 9688

Babytalk
020 8876 4448

JoeyCo
7 Bovingdon Road, SW6. 020 7736 0938
julierosengren@onetel.net.uk

The New Learning Centre
211 Sumatra Road, NW6. 020 7794 0321
tnlc@dial.pipex.com

Parenting Matters
31 Windermere Avenue London, N3.
020 834 32045
babyjake@ntlworld.com

Positive Parenting Publications
First floor, 2a South Street, Gosport,
Hampshire. 01705 528787
www.parenting.org.uk
Parenting skills resource

"Which part of 'No' don't you understand, darling?"

parks & playgrounds

(see also adventure playgrounds, nature reserves, one o'clock clubs, outings)

E3
Mile End Park
Green Bridge

Victoria Park, Old Ford Road
One o'clock club, adventure playground, plus two playgrounds, deer enclosure, boating lake, café and paddling pool

E5
Springfield Park
Café, one o'clock club, pond

N2
Cherry Tree Woods
Woodland, football area, good playground, café and toilets

N4
Finsbury Park
Boating lake, adventure playground, climbing frames, one o'clock club

N5
Highbury Fields
Good equipment for all ages. Helter skelter, huge slide, seesaw tyres (good for adults too – when no-one's looking!), water play area, sandpit with toys, cycling roundabout

N6
Highgate Woods, Muswell Hill Road
Boating lake, adventure playground, climbing frames, one o'clock club. Link with Highgate via Parkland Walk (buggy-able)

Waterlow Park
Three duck ponds, flowerbeds, squirrels. Tiny under five playground. Café

N8
Campsbourne
At the foot of Alexandra Park. Tyre swings, slide, playhouse, rockers, climbing frame

Priory Park
Tarmac area for bikes and roller-skates. Enclosed playground with swings, paddling pool, refreshment kiosk

Stationers Park
Ducks, picnic tables, enclosed playground

N10
Queen's Wood
Natural woodland, jungle walkway for 5-9yrs. Café, ecology centre

Coldfall Woods
Natural woodland area

N13
Broomfield Park
Broomfield Lane, Palmers Green. 020 8379 3722. Good playground, several complex structures

N16
Clissold Park
Good playground, paddling pool, animals, one o'clock club. Butterfly tunnel. Cafe open all year

N17
Bruce Castle Park
Lordship Lane. Tarmac trike area, toddler swings, climbing frame, rope climbing pyramid

Downhills Park & Recreation Ground
Park with squirrels. Well-designed play equipment

Lordship Lane Recreation Ground
Lake with ducks. Playground with swings, etc

Tower Gardens
Risley Avenue. Plenty of equipment, large sandpit, swings, climbing structures

N22
Alexandra Palace and Park
Alexandra Palace Way, Wood Green. Boating lake, paddling pool, sandpit, playground, deer and llama paddocks. Famous firework display in November

NW1
Camden Square
Good adventure playground for older children manned both after school and on Saturdays

Cantelowes Park
Osney Street. Playground, skateboard/BMX ramp

p

Visit us at
www.babydirectory.com

parks & playgrounds (cont.)

Lisson Gardens
Lisson Street.
Small-scale toddler equipment

Primrose Hill
Useful adjunct to zoo visit. Good secure playground, plentiful roundabouts. Loos. Good helter skelter slide. Unusual play structure. Sandpit. Overlooks aviary

Regents Park
Boating lake, three good adventure playgrounds. You can see some animals if you walk round the outside of the zoo. Poor cafés

Rochester Terrace Gardens
Kentish Town Road.
Playground for toddlers and for larger kids

Talacre Open Space
Prince of Wales Road.
Recently restored gardens and playground

NW3
Hampstead Heath
Kite flying. Playgrounds at Constantine Road end. One o'clock club weekdays. Swimming pools in summer

NW5
Parliament Hill
Highgate Road, Kentish Town.
Part of Hampstead Heath with supervised traditional playground, playpark and one o'clock club. Kites, views. Supervised playground near Savernake Road, with large sandpit, paddling pool May-Sept

NW8
Roundwood Park
Harlesden Road.
Playground, birdcages, good café

St John's Wood Parish Park
Good climbing frames, swings, etc.

Violet Hill
Off Abbey Gardens.
Helter skelter, swings, roundabout

NW10 ☺
Queens Park
Roundwood Park, Halesden Road.
Clean paddling pool. Excellent equipment including wooden castle, climbing pole, huge sandpit, helter skelter. One o'clock club. Friendly café. Small farm with rabbits and chickens.

NW11
Golders Hill Park
West Heath Avenue.
Flower gardens, duck and flamingo ponds. Deer, wallabies and exotic birds in small animal section. Large sandpit and climbing structure. Good but busy café

SE1
Archbishops Park
Lambeth Palace Road.
Playground with slides, train

Leather Market Gardens
Western Street

SE5
Burgess Park
Camberwell Road. Playground, wooden animals, paddling pool

Myatts Field
Knatchbull Road. One o'clock club

Ruskin Park
Playground, paddling pool, one o'clock club

SE10
Greenwich Park
King William Way.
Great views, Meridian Line, surrounded by museums, boats and all things maritime

SE11
Kennington Park
Playground, one o'clock club

SE22
Dulwich Park
Aviary and boating lakes (lots of ducks) good children's play area, recently refurbished. Dogs off leash only on outer circle. One o'clock club. Parking free. Café

SE24
Brockwell Park
Dulwich Road.
Playground, one o'clock club, aviary, sandpit

SE26
Crystal Palace
Worth the occasional trip. Children's Zoo. Terrific sporting facilities. Large open space. Dinosaur trail. Easy parking (big distances to walk). Pony rides. One o'clock club. Good playground

Sydenham Wells Park
Wells Park Road, Sydenham

SW1
St James's Park
Pelicans fed at 3pm, bandstand, playground

Causton Street
Sandpit, paddling pool, train, playhouse

Green Park
Good for picnics

SW3
St Luke's Gardens
Sydney Street
Enclosed play area with swings and rockers. Small adventure play structure, plank bridge and slide. Benches and toilets

SW4
Clapham Common
Grandison Road and Windmill Drive sides have playgrounds with sandpits. Café near Nightingale Road. Paddling pool opposite Clapham Common tube

SW6
Normand Park
Behind Fulham Pools. Basic slides, playhouses, trikes occasionally put out. Tough kids (and mothers). Lots of fag-ends

Bishop's Park ☺
Large playground. One o'clock club. Enclosed swing area. Two very good climbing frames, and a nice train. Usually a good selection of bikes and tunnels, a large sand pit and a quiet clean paddling pool. Access to the riverside walk. Small very basic café

South Park
Good playground

SW8
Larkhall Park

SW10
Cremorne Gardens
Lots Road. Small paddling pool

SW11
Battersea Park ☺
One o'clock club. Also children's zoo (*see zoos*). Boating, good adventure playgrounds. Pond and impressive group of fountains

SW13
Castelnau Recreation Ground
Washington Road/Barnes Avenue. Large paddling pool. Playground

Palewell Common
East Sheen.
Playground, round clean paddling pool adjoining open space for football etc. Merry-go-round, ice-cream kiosk

Vine Road Recreation Ground
Vine Road, Barnes.
Playground, large paddling pool

Mortlake Green
Old-fashioned style swings and slide

SW16
Streatham Common
Rockery, playground, padding pool, café

SW17
Tooting Bec Common
Good playground, pond, café

SW18
St George's Park
Mapleton Road.
Animal enclosure, playgrounds, one o'clock club

SW19
Cannizaro Park
Sculptures, woodlands, azaleas

Dundonald Park
Dundonald Road.
Playground, paddling pool

John Innes Park
Mostyn Road. Ornamental gardens

Quicks Road Recreation Ground
off Haydon's Road.
Large playground

Wandsworth Common
Nature trail

Wellington Road Recreation Ground
Playground

parks & playgrounds (cont.)

Wimbledon Common
Car parks in Windmill Road, Camp Road. Real windmill

Wimbledon Park
Car parks in Wimbledon Park Road, Revelstoke Road.
Lake, two playgrounds, sandpit, paddling pool. Café

SW20
Canon Hill Common/Joseph Hood Recreation Ground
Pond, playground

Cottenham Park
Melbury Gardens. Playground

TW1
Marble Hill House
Richmond Road. 020 8892 5115
Adventure playground, one o'clock club, café (Mar-Oct)

TW7
Osterley Park
Jersey Road, Isleworth. 020 8232 5050
Extensive grounds of large house. Good teas in old stables. Lake, gardens and large "wild" green areas. Cows and horses in surrounding fields. Great bluebells (worth coming from afar).

TW8
Syon Park
Brentford. 020 8560 0883
Lake, train in summer. Entry charge

Boston Manor Park
Boston Manor Road, Brentford.
020 8560 5441
Playground cunningly situated virtually under the motorway. Nature trail, pond, scarey woodlands and copious dog mess. Annual Civil War battle re-enactments

TW9
Richmond Park
Off the A3. Largest royal park in London. Wide open spaces, trees, lots of deer, lakes, horses etc. Also the Isabella Plantation, an enclosed area, beautiful especially in spring

Royal Botanic Gardens
Kew. 020 8940 1171
Worth the price of entry even in bleak midwinter to gain entrance to palm houses. Good cafes, wonderful aquarium (down a buggy unfriendly spiral stair in the Palm House). No balls or dogs

W1
Hyde Park
Little playground. Views of horses passing. Lots of ducks. Boats on Serpentine. Paddling pool at Lido, slides, café, fishing, adventure playground

W2
Diana Princess of Wales Memorial Playground
Kensington Gardens.
New and hugely popular ship playground. Prepare to queue to enter on hot summer days. Old Elfin Oak, Peter Pan statue still there too…

Paddington Gardens
Moxon Street.
Two play areas. Splendid tall slide, good complex structures. One o'clock club, café

W3
Acton Park
Uxbridge Road.
Playground, play centre for under 5s

Springfield Gardens
Horn Lane.
Small playground with cowboy wagon, tennis courses

W4
Dukes Meadow
Off Great Chertsey Road, behind Chiswick New Pool.
Secret and empty playground. Good climbing structure and swings, and unusual elastic climbing frame to have a boing on. Beware broken glass

Chiswick House
Burlington Lane. 020 8995 0508
Great woodland with hidden pathways,
possibly one of the slowest cafés in town
(w/e only in winter). Chiswick
Extravaganza held on summer Bank
Holiday very child-friendly

W5
Gunnersbury Park
Popes Lane.
Two playgrounds, one for under 5s, larger
one good for toddlers and older kids too.
Recently refurbished café, boating pond,
good museum

Hanger Hill Park
Hillcrest Road.
Good playground. Hill for tobogganing,
pitch and putt

Lammas Park
Northfield Avenue/Church Lane.
Wildlife area, open fields for football

W5
Walpole Park
Mattock Lane.
Aviary with rabbits and guinea pigs, small
playground, summer café

W6
Brook Green
Recent face-lift. New structures with rope
bridges, sandpit, etc

Ravenscourt Park
020 8741 2051
Three areas for children. Good swings,
slides, balancing equipment. One o'clock
club. Unusual wooden structures. Dog-free
zones. Excellent paddling pool. Sandpit.
Slow café

W7
Brent Lodge River Park
Church Road, Hanwell. 020 8758 5019
Aka Bunny Park, with two playgrounds,
small zoo, café

W8/W14 ☺
Holland Park
Abbotsbury Road.
Sandpits, one o'clocks, woodland, excellent
café, Japanese garden, rabbits, peacocks,
sculptures, altogether wonderful

W10
Emslie Horniman Pleasance
Bosworth Road.
Victorian gardens a la Teletubbies. Also
lovely quiet gardens.

Queen's Park Gardens
Ilbert Street.
Playground for under 7s with good
equipment

Meanwhile Gardens
Elkstone Road.
Sandpit, paddling pool, small castle,
crocodile. Under 5s drop-in centre

W11
Avondale Park
Walmer Road.
Small, containable. Enclosed toddler
playground (no baby swings); all the usual
playground equipment. Wildlife pond

W11
Colville Gardens
Small enclosed toddlers playground. Useful
for locals -not worth visiting otherwise

Memorial Park ☺
St Mark's Road.
Clean paddling pool. Standard play
equipment. Sandpit. Excellent one o'clock
club. Basic café

W12
Hammersmith Park
North end of Frithville Gardens.
Landscaped park, adventure playground,
busy little paddling pool

Wendell Park
Small local park and playground

Wormwood Scrubs
Standard play area with one unusual
complex play structure

WC1
Coram's Fields
93 Guildford Street.
Dog-free grass, pets corner (sheep, goats).
Tyre swing, cable run, paddling pool,
sandpit. Refurbished.
"Immaculately clean," Reader's comment

Phoenix Gardens
Woodland gardens, with small climbing
frame, mini fort

Drury Lane (near Aldwych)
Sandpit, slide, roundabout

party catering

(see also cakes, party entertainers, party equipment)

Canapes Gastronomiques
34 Cholmley Gardens, Aldred Road, NW6.
020 7794 2017

Annie Fry Catering Ltd
134 Lots Road, SW10. 020 7351 4333

KPC Organic (Kensington Provision Company)
020 7386 7778
Organic

Mallard Catering
84 Bellenden Road, SE15. 020 7642 5495

Nikki Brown Catering
020 8336 0395

Puddleduck Parties
10 Faulkner House, Horne Way, SW15.
020 8788 7240

party entertainers

Art 4 Fun
See advert under party venues

Creative Wiz Kids
020 7794 6797
1-9yrs

Crêchendo Children's Parties
020 8772 8140
www.crechendo.com

Ink Tank
020 7639 5611
SE. Also art classes

Little Blisters
020 8948 3874

Mexicolore
020 7622 9577
ian.mursell@btinternet.com
www.pinata.co.uk
See advert on page 169

Monkey Music
01582 766464
See advert on page 95

Pippin Puppets
020 8348 4055

Twizzle Parties
020 8392 6788

Action Stations
020 7263 8468

Adam Ant
020 8959 1045

p

party entertainers (cont.)

Amanda's Action Kids
020 8933 1269
See advert on page 98

Blueberry Playsongs Parties
020 8677 6871
www.blueberry.clara.co.uk

Bob Thingummybob
020 8907 4606

Boo Boo
020 7727 3817
www.mr-booboo.co.uk

The Buzz Bus
020 8878 3450

Clowning Glory
020 8440 5869
4-12yrs

Creative Faces
020 8444 4489

David Brooker
020 8949 5035
Punch and Judy, Magical Clown

Diane's Puppets
020 7820 9466
1yr+

Fancy Faces
020 7372 1045
fancyfaces@emilj.globalnet.co.uk

Fizzie Lizzie
020 7723 3877

Happy Puzzle Company
0800 376 3727
6yrs+

Happy Times
020 8207 3737

Impeyan Productions
01992 446211
www.impeyan.co.uk
Animals, clown

JC Disco
020 8561 5919

Jellybean Julie
020 8896 1235

Jolly Roger Entertainments
020 8902 3373
Many different kinds

Juggling John
020 8672 8468
www.juggle.co.uk

Kidspace Clubs
01932 340098
Stickfings@aol.com
Art and craft party

Little Entertainers
020 8948 3874
entertainers@intune.co.uk

Lydie
020 7622 2540
Beauty & Beast, bilingual French

Magician Lee Warren
020 8670 2729

Mini Makeovers
020 8398 6769
www.minimakeovers.com
6-14yrs

Mr & Mrs Squash
020 8808 1415

Mr G.
020 8907 0509

Mr Toots
020 8366 6051
Magic, balloons

Mrs Marvel
020 8679 0917
www.marvellous-productions.com
3-12yrs

Mrs Roundabout
SE. 020 8778 3287

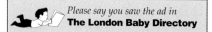

Nellie's young@art parties
020 7428 7600

Netti the Clown
020 8451 2389

Nick Spellman
01992 446211
www.nickspellman.com

Partyplay
020 7737 6817
5yrs+

Pekko's Puppets
020 8579 7651

Pizzazz
01225 333093

Pro-Active Leisure Children's Parties
020 8446 3132

Puddleduck Parties
020 8788 7240

Smartie Artie
01582 483977
www.smartieartie.com

Splodge
020 7350 1473
splodge@virgin.net

Sports Workshop Ltd
020 8659 4561

party equipment

(see also fancy dress, party catering, party entertainers)

Bounce Away
020 8788 2647
Bouncy castles, tables, chairs for hire

Crêchendo Children's Parties
020 8772 8140
www.crechendo.com
See advert under party entertainers

party equipment (cont.)

Mexicolore
020 7622 9577
www.pinata.co.uk
Piñatas (papier mâché animals exploding
with sweets) delivered around the country
See advert on page 169

Bouncing Kids
020 8998 1008

Games Hire
01753 893630
More than just bouncy stuff

Jumping Jacks
020 8579 6320
Bouncy castles

Partyworks
0870 240 2103

mail order:

Party Angels
01908 583732
www.partyangels.co.uk

Party Pieces
01635 201844

Party Zone
01277 226999
www.partyzone.co.uk

retail:

N3
Surprises
82 Ballards Lane. 020 8343 4200

NW5
Party Party
11 Southampton Road. 020 7267 9084

NW6
Oscar's Den
127-129 Abbey Road. 020 7328 6683

SE9
Crocodile Club
STC Sports Club, Ivor Grove, New Eltham.
020 8461 1351

SE20
One Stop Party Shop
67 High Street, Penge. 020 8676 7900

SW1
Just Balloons
127 Wilton Road. 020 7434 3039

SW6
Circus Circus
176 Wandsworth Bridge Road. 020 7731
4128

Non Stop Party Shop
694 Fulham Road. 020 7384 1491
www.nonstopparty.co.uk

SW11
It's My Party
23 Webbs Road. 020 7350 2763

SW18
Balloon and Kite Company
613 Garratt Lane. 020 8946 5962
www.balloon-kite.co.uk

W1
American Party Store
16 Woodstock Street. 020 7493 2678

W4
Party Plus
4 Acton Lane, Chiswick Park. 020 8987 8404

W5
Carnival
129 Little Ealing Lane. 020 8567 3210

W8
Non Stop Party Shop
214-216 Kensington High Street.
020 7937 7200
www.nonstopparty.co.uk

W10
Purple Planet
318-320 Portobello Road. 020 8969 4119

Art 4 Fun
Tel: 020-8-99-44-800
EMAIL: Paint@Art4Fun.com
WEB & VIRTUAL STORE: www.Art4Fun.com
PARTIES: Birthday parties, office functions, hen nights, brides book, and other special occasions or
DROP IN ANY TIME and paint a ceramic, wood, plaster, glass, fabric, paper item or make a mosaic
WORKSHOPS: Ask about our Little Artists Club
ALL OUR MATERIALS ARE LEAD-FREE & NON-TOXIC
Items from £1.00 and up
£3.95 studio fee per person painting - paint all day!
NOTTING HILL: 196 Kensington Park Road, W11
WEST HAMPSTEAD: 172 West End Lane, NW6
MUSWELL HILL: 212 Fortis Green Road, N10
CHISWICK: 444 Chiswick High, W4

Stop & see what we offer

paternity testing

Cellmark Diagnostics
01235 528 609

party venues

Try arts centres, church halls, farms, indoor adventure playcentres, leisure centres and swimming pools.

Art 4 Fun Venues
196 Kensington Park Road, W11.
172 West End Lane, NW6.
212 Fortis Green Road, N10.
444 Chiswick High, W4.
020 8994 4800
www.Art4Fun.com

Halls for Hire in Camden
Cindex Online. 020 7860 5974
£3. "Invaluable". Reader's comment

Minimarkee
20 Bradmore Park Road, W6.
020 8741 2777
Keep the rain off your garden and the little perishers out of your house

personal trainers

(see also exercise classes, health clubs with crèches)

Academy of Personal Fitness
020 8699 6688
www.lapf.co.uk
See advert under exercise

Gillian Leslie
020 8992 8399
See advert under exercise

Revolution Health
0958 464770
See advert under exercise

Momentum Fitness
020 8772 1346

N6/N8/N10/N14
Anne Marie Millard
020 8365 3320

NW3/NW6
Alison Lidstone
077699 71331

W4
Rosemary Newman
44 Hartington Road. 020 8994 0369
rosemary_newman@hotmail.com

p

personality changes in pregnancy

Is it true? Yes, blame the hormones.
Is it reversible? Supposedly.
Will my memory ever return to
pre-pregnant levels?
*See page xxxx [note to ed. remember to fill in on
final draft]*

photographers specialising in babies & children

Sophie Carr
3 Burnaby Gardens, W4.
020 8995 0637

Tia May
23 Fabian Road, SW6.
020 7610 0465

Robin Farquhar-Thomson
15 Albert Bridge Road, SW11.
020 7622 3630

Diana Vowles
38 Keslake Road, NW6.
020 8968 8136
www.dianavowles.co.uk

www.photoalbum.co.uk
Internet photo album

Roz Allibone
0780 871 9881
www.rozallibone.com

Alice Auster-Rhodes
0779 886994

Michael Bassett
020 7326 4849

Mark Dyer
020 7564 8826

Desi Fontaine Studios
020 8878 4348

Paul Hine
020 7240 5020

David and Pia Randall-Goddard
020 8693 3925

Gwen Shabka
020 7386 7007
www.shabkaphotography.com

Diana Vowles

Naturalistic black and white portraits of children

38 Keslake Road
London NW6 6DL

tel
020 8968 8136

email
info@dianavowles.co.uk

website
www.dianavowles.co.uk

Janet Sherbow
020 7384 1114

Zeit Light
07939 288447

physiotherapists

N10
Susana Weiner back problems
1 Pages Hill. 020 8444 4284

South West
Sue Lewis
020 8946 8561

SW10
The Chelsea Practice for Physio & Sports Injuries
186 Fulham Road. 020 7351 9918

SW11
The Battersea Practice
40 Webbs Road. 020 7228 2141

SW12
Physiotherapy for Babies & Children
133 Thurleigh Road. 020 7207 4234
www. kikisclinic.com

W1
Portland Hospital
205-209 Great Portland Street.
020 7580 4400
www.theportlandhospital.com

The Chartered Society of Physiotherapists
14 Bedford Row, WC1. 020 7306 6666
Contact for details of qualified physios in your area

p

planning

$\mathcal{The}$ $\mathcal{Forward}$ $\mathcal{Planner}$

Reproduced by kind permission of **The Dodo Pad**©
"The perfect antidote to organisational chaos".
See advertisement under gifts

playgroups

Contact the Pre-School Learning Alliance
on 020 7833 0991 for up-to-date information
on your local playgroup. For non-PLA
playgroups, contact the Under 8s section at
your local council *(see councils)*.

Come and check us out

portraits

(see also photographers)

Naomi Clements-Wright
020 7228 9699

Pamela Lloyd-Jones
020 8993 5697

Julian Murray
01932 562611 ext 3050

postnatal support

*(see also breastfeeding advice, helplines:
postnatal advice, mother & baby groups)*

National Childbirth Trust (NCT)
Alexandra House, Oldham Terrace,
London W3. 0870 444 8707

W3/W5
Postnatal and Discussion Group
020 8992 8399
See advert on page 41

Full Time Mothers
PO Box 186. London SW3 5RF
www.fulltimemothers.org

pram & buggy repair

For details of major manufacturers ask at
the shop where you bought the pram. They
should deal with any serious problems.

N22
London Nursery Supplies
Hardy Passage, Berners Road.
020 8889 3003

SW15
Barnes Buggy Repair Centre
278 Upper Richmond Road. 020 8785 2022

premature babies

Bliss:
National Charity for the New Born
020 7820 9471

psychologists & psychotherapists

Association of Child Psychotherapists
020 8458 1609
acap@dial.pipex.com

Blackhill
209 Pitshanger Lane, W5. 020 8566 7539
bglclinic@aol.com

Child Consultants
27a Harley Place, W1. 020 7637 3177

Rosemary Newsom-Davis
London Medical Centre,
144 Harley Street, W1. 020 7935 0023

pubs with gardens or playrooms

E6
Winsor House
Woolwich Manor Way, Beckton.
020 7511 3853

N1
Duke of Cambridge
30 St Peter's Street. 020 7359 3066
Organic too!

SE10
Ashburnham Arms
25 Ashburnham Grove. 020 8692 2007

SW4
Bread and Roses
68 Clapham Manor Street. 020 7498 1779
Back garden, toys

SW13
The Red Lion
Castelnau Street. 020 8748 2984
Playground. Back room

Coach & Horses
Barnes High Street. 020 8876 2695
Separate room on Sunday.
Garden "packed with kids"

SW15
Green Man
Putney Heath. 020 8788 8096
Swings in garden

Robin Hood Pub
Kingston Vale. 020 8546 4316

SW20
Emma Hamilton
328 Kingston Road. 020 8540 5093

W6
Black Lion
2 Black Lion Terrace. 020 8748 2639

The Queen's Head
Brook Green

pushchairs: all-terrain

p

Pegasus Pushchairs Ltd
Westbridge, Tavistock, Devon.
01822 618077
www.allterrain.co.uk

PW Trading Ltd
PO Box 506, St Albans, Herts AL4 0LT.
01727 811 221

■ *Retail*
SW6
Baby List Company
The Broomhouse, 50 Sulivan Road.
020 7371 5145
See advert on page 149

SW15
Little Green Earthlets
163 Lower Richmond Road. 020 8780 3075
See advert on page 111

rattles

Plate, Rattle and Roll
38 Burwood Road, Northampton.
01604 406320
www.babies-rattles.co.uk

Tweedledum and Tweedledee
Agreed to have a battle;
For Tweedledum said Tweedledee
Had spoiled his nice new rattle.

Lewis Carroll

reflexologists

(see also complementary health)

The British School of Reflexology
The Holistic Healing Centre,
92 Sheering Road, Old Harlow.
01279 429 060

British Reflexology Association
Monks Orchard, Whitbourne, Worcester.
01886 821207

N/NW
Harriet Tully
0956 900524

SW3
Heather Guerrini
020 7352 0245

SW18
Emma Bisdee
020 8870 1565

W4
Lizzie Hibbitt
020 8994 1076

registration of births

You have 6 weeks to decide on "its" name
before you must register your baby with
your local Registry Office.

Visit us at
www.babydirectory.com

restaurants: child-friendly

(see also pubs)

These restaurants usually have high chairs
and changing facilities. Some also offer
crayons, toys or entertainers at Sunday
lunch times

N1
Maremma
11-13 Theburton Street. 020 7226 9400

Santa Fe
75 Upper Street. 020 7288 2288

Tiger Lil's
270 Upper Street. 020 7226 1118

N4
La Porchetta Pizzeria
147 Stroud Green Road. 020 7281 2892

N6
Idaho
13 North Hill. 020 8341 6633

N8
Banners
21 Park Road. 020 8348 2930

Florians
4 Topsfield Parade, Middle Lane.
020 8348 8348

N10
Caffe Uno
348 Muswell Hill Broadway. 020 8883 4463
Crayons, kiddy packs.

Down the Hatch
148 Colney Hatch Lane. 020 8444 7782

N16
The Cooler
67 Stoke Newington Church Street.
020 7275 7266

NW3
Benihana
100 Avenue Road. 020 7586 7118

Maxwell's Restaurant
76 Heath Street. 020 7794 5450

NW7
TGI Friday
Pentaria Retail Park, Watford Way,
Mill Hill. 020 8203 9779

NW8
Don Pepe
99 Frampton Street. 020 7262 3834

SE1
Bella Pasta
35 Tooley Street. 020 7407 5267

Gourmet Pizza Company
Gabriels Wharf, 56 Upper Ground.
020 7928 3188

Pizzeria Castello
20 Walworth Road, Elephant & Castle.
020 7703 2556

SE19
Joanna's
56 Westow Hill. 020 8670 4052

SE22
Spaghetti Western
121 Lordship Lane, East Dulwich.
020 8299 2372
Crayons, Sunday newspapers

Blue Mountain Café
18 North Cross Road. 020 8299 6953

SE24
Café Provencal
4-6 Half Moon Lane, Herne Hill.
020 7978 9228

SW1
O Sole Mio
39 Churton Street. 020 7976 6887

SW3
Big Easy
332 King's Road. 020 7352 4071

Browns
114 Draycott Ave. 020 7584 5359

Calzone
352a Kings Road. 020 7352 9790
Colouring

Henry J Beans
195-7 King's Road. 020 7352 9255

Le Shop
329 King's Road. 020 7352 3891

SW4
Newton's
35 Abbeville Road, Clapham Common
South Side. 020 8673 0977

SW6
Blue Elephant
4-6 Fulham Broadway. 020 7385 6595

Tootsies
177 New King's Road. 020 7736 4023

SW7
Café Rouge
102 Old Brompton Road. 020 7373 2403
and other branches

Pizza Chelsea
93 Pelham Street. 020 7584 4788

Pizza Organic
20 Old Brompton Road. 020 7589 9613

Francofill
1 Old Brompton Road. 020 7584 0087

SW8
Le Bouchon Lyonnais
38 Queenstown Road. 020 7622 2618

SW10
Deals
Chelsea Harbour. 020 7795 1001

La Famiglia
7 Langton Street. 020 7351 0761

SW11
The Boiled Egg & Soldiers
63 Northcote Road. 020 7223 4894

Le Bouchon Bordelais
9 Battersea Rise. 020 7738 0307
Free crèche

Glaister's Garden Bistro
8-10 Northcote Road. 020 7924 6699

The Inebriated Newt
172 Northcote Road. 020 7223 1637

Ransome's Dock
35 Parkgate Road. 020 7223 1611

SW13
Browns
201 Castlenau Road. 020 8748 4486

SW14
The Naked Turtle
505 Upper Richmond Road. 020 8878 1995
Entertainer Sunday lunch

SW15
Moomba
5 Lacy Road. 020 8785 9151

SW17
Pitcher and Piano
11 Bellevue Road. 020 8767 6982

Visit us at
www.babydirectory.com

restaurants: child-friendly (cont.)

SW19
Gourmet Pizza Company
Merton Abbey Mills. 020 8545 0310
Sunday entertainers. No bookings Sunday

W1
Amalfi
31 Old Compton Street. 020 7437 7284

Browns
47 Maddox Street. 020 7491 4565

Down Mexico Way
25 Swallow Street. 020 7437 9895

Gaylord
79 Mortimer Street. 020 7580 3615

Giraffe
6-8 Blandford Street. 020 7935 2333
Also in N1, NW3

Momo
25 Heddon Street. 020 7434 4040
Sat & Sun lunchtime kids club

Rainforest Café
20 Shaftesbury Avenue. 020 7434 3111

La Reash Cous-Cous House
23-24 Greek Street. 020 7439 1063

Signor Zilli
41 Dean Street. 020 7734 3924

Yo! Sushi
52 Poland Street. 020 7287 0443
Also at Harvey Nichols, Selfridges, 02
Centre, Farringdon Road, Finchley Road.
Baby chopsticks, crayons, kids club

W2
Mandarin Kitchen
14-16 Queensway. 020 7727 9468

W3
Honey for the Bears
167 The Vale. 020 8749 9581

W4
Mongolian Barbecue
1-3 Acton Lane. 020 8995 0575
Other branches in Kensington, Wimbledon,
Covent Garden

W5
Pizza Organic
100 Pitshanger Lane. 020 8998 6878

Old Orleans
26-42 Bond Street. 020 8579 7413

W6
Deals
Bradmore House, Queen Caroline Street.
020 8563 1001
Crayons, high chairs, kids menu

W8
Phoenicia
11-13 Abingdon Road. 020 7937 0120

W11
Julie's Restaurant
135 Portland Road. 020 7229 8331
Crèche on Sunday

Tootsies
120 Holland Park Avenue. 020 7229 8567
and other branches

WC1
Charoscuro at Town House
24 Coptic Street. 020 7636 2731

WC2
Brown's Restaurant
82-84 St Martin's Lane. 020 7497 5050

Café in the Crypt
Crypt of St Martin-in-the-Fields,
Duncannon Street. 020 7839 4342

Café Pacifico
5 Langley Street. 020 7379 7728

Haagen-Dazs on the Square
14 Leicester Square. 020 7287 9577
and other branches

Luna Nuova
22 Shorts Gardens, off Neal Street.
020 7379 3336

Maxwell's
8-9 James Street. 020 7836 0303

Porters
17 Henrietta Street. 020 7836 6466

Rock Garden
6 The Piazza, Covent Garden. 020 7240 3961

TGI Friday
6 Bedford Street. 020 7379 0585
and other branches

Wolfe's
30 Great Queen Street. 020 7831 4442

re-training

Been out of the office for a year or two? Worried that you are hopelessly out of date? Need a refresher course, or just a bit of mental stimulation after all that posseting and nappy talk? Check out Adult Education classes (some offer crèches), the Open University, your Local Authority careers advice. Look in local papers, the library, buy a copy of *Floodlight* (available at newsagents) for all London course listings.

Kumon Educational
0800 854 714
www.kumon.co.uk
See advert on page 192

riding

Many stables do not recommend riding for under 5s

E6
Newham Riding School
Docklands Equestrian Centre,
2 Claps Gate Lane. 020 7511 3917

E10
Lea Valley Riding Centre
Lea Bridge Road. 020 8556 2629

E12
Aldersbrook Riding School
Empress Avenue, Manor Park.
020 8530 4648
3yrs+

N12
London Equestrian Centre
Lulington Garth, Woodside Park.
020 8349 1345
Café. 2yrs+

N14
Trent Park Equestrian Centre
Bramley Road. 020 8363 9005

SE21
Dulwich Riding School
Dulwich Common. 020 8693 2944

SW7
Kensington Stables
11 Elvaston Mews. 020 7589 2299

SW15
Roehampton Gate Equestrian Centre
Priory Lane, Richmond Park. 020 8876 7089

Stag Lodge Stables
Robin Hood Gate, Richmond Park.
020 8974 6066

SW19
Deen City Farm
39 Windsor Avenue, Merton Abbey.
020 8543 5858
4yrs+

Ridgeway Stables
93 Ridgeway, Wimbledon Village.
020 8946 7400
3¹/2yrs+

Wimbledon Village Stables
24 High Street. 020 8946 8579

W2
Hyde Park & Kensington Stables
63 Bathurst Mews. 020 7723 2813

Ross Nye's
8 Bathurst Mews. 020 7262 3791
6yrs+

W5
Ealing Riding School
17-19 Gunnersbury Avenue. 020 8992 3808
5yrs+

W10
Westways Riding Stables
20 Stable Way. 020 8964 2140

W12
Wormwood Scrubs Pony Centre
Woodmans Mews, Scrubs Lane.
020 8740 0573

rocking horses

(see also nursery furniture)

Edward's Attic: hand crafted gifts
020 8325 8230
edwardsattic@cwcom.net

Robert Mullis
01793 813583
robert@rockinghorse.freeserve.co.uk

CHILDproofers

Making homes safer for babies and children
- Survey of dangers in your home
- Written report and recommendations
- Supply and fitting of products as required
- Made-to-measure safety solutions

020 7433 3382
info@childproofers.co.uk

LITTLE ANGELS

**Baby Proofing & Child Proofing
is the Greatest Achievement in Child Safety
in the UK since the car seat**
Little Angels can eliminate the time consuming and tedious work
of advising and **fitting** accident prevention and monitoring
equipment which could **protect** your child from serious accidents
or injuries in the home.
Call for a free brochure on **020 7373 2070**
E-mail us for advice on: **littleangels.babyproofing@virgin.net**

safety advice

Baby Safety Harness & Nets
Helmar Straps, Stourbridge, West
Midlands. 01384 422922
www.helmar-straps.com
Manufacturers who will supply Baby
Directory readers direct.

**Child Accident Prevention Trust
(CAPT)**
18-20 Farringdon Lane, London EC1.
020 7608 3828

Childproofers Ltd
020 7433 3382
www.childproofers.com

www.childalert.co.uk
See advert under nanny agencies

Little Angels Baby Proofing Service Ltd
39 Cadogan Square, SW1.
020 7245 6226 / 07944 632 942
safeangels@aol.com

school consultants

ISIS (Independent Schools Information
Service) and Gabbitas can supply
information on private schools in your area.
Both produce books and information
covering the schools in your area, and also
offer further consultancy services.

Gabbitas Educational Consultants
Carrington House,
126-130 Regent Street, W1.
020 7734 0161
www.gabbitas.co.uk

ISIS London & South-East
Grosvenor Gardens House,
35-37 Grosvenor Gardens, SW1.
020 7798 1560
www.isis.org.uk / southeast
See advert on page 182

school runs

**The School Mule
www.schoolmule.co.uk**

School Run Company
273 Eversholt Street, NW1. 020 7387 1707
4yrs+

Six 2 16
3 Irwin Gardens, NW10. 020 8830 2255

Check out updated listings

schools, preparatory and pre-prep

(see also helplines: education, nurseries, school consultants)

For a list of state schools in your area, contact your local council *(see councils)*. The following schools have a nursery section.

E4
Normanhurst School
68-74 Station Road, Chingford.
020 8529 4307
Co-ed 2-16yrs

E18
Snaresbrook College
75 Woodford Road. 020 8989 2394
Co-ed 3-11yrs

N1
Children's House
77 Elmore Street. 020 7354 2113
2¹/₂-5yrs

St Paul's Steiner Project
1 St Paul's Road, Islington. 020 7226 4454
3-9yrs. Also toddler and playgroups

N2
Annemount School
18 Holne Chase. 020 8455 2132

Kerem School
Norrice Lea. 020 8455 0909
4-11yrs

N5
Primrose Montessori School
Congregational Church, Highbury
Quadrant. 020 7359 8985
2-11yrs

N6
Channing School
Highgate. 020 8340 2328
Girls 4-18yrs

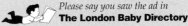

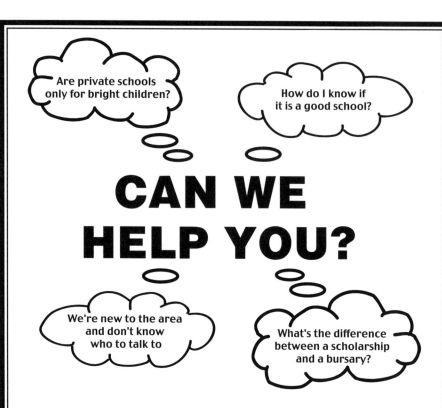

ISIS – the Independent Schools Information Service was set up specifically to help parents find information about independent schools in their area. Our consultants have a wealth of personal experience. They have worked in independent schools, their children attend independent schools and they regularly visit the schools in London and the South East region. Whether you are short of time or just need someone to talk to, join the hundreds of families who have found the support and information they needed through our consultancy service.

Tel: 020 7798 1560
Fax: 020 7798 1561
E-mail: southeast@isis.org.uk
www.isis.org.uk/southeast

ISIS London & South East

schools, preparatory and pre-prep (cont.)

Highgate Pre-Preparatory School
7 Bishopswood Road. 020 8340 9196
Co-ed 3-7yrs. Boys 8-13yrs. Part of
Highgate School, Junior School at
Cholmeley House, 3 Bishopswood Road,
N6 4PL. 020 8340 9193

N10
Norfolk House Prep School
10 Muswell Avenue. 020 8883 4584
Co-ed 4-11yrs

Prince's Avenue School
5 Prince's Avenue. 020 8444 4399
Co-ed 5-7yrs

N12
Woodside Park International School
49 Woodside Avenue. 020 8368 3777
Co-ed 2-18yrs

N14
Salcombe Prep School
224-226 Chase Side, Southgate.
020 8441 5282
Co-ed 4-11yrs

N21
Keble Prep School
Wades Hill, Winchmore Hill. 020 8360 3359
Boys 4-13yrs

Palmers Green High School
Hoppers Road, Winchmore Hill.
020 8886 1135
Girls 3-16yrs

NW1
The Cavendish School
179 Arlington Road. 020 7485 1958
Girls 3-11yrs

NW2
Mulberry House School
7 Minster Road. 020 8452 7340
Co-ed 2-8yrs

NW3
Devonshire House School
69 Fitzjohn's Avenue. 020 7435 1916
2-11yrs Girls, 2-13yrs Boys. Follow-on from
Oak Tree Nursery

Hall School
23 Crossfield Road. 020 7722 1700
Boys 5-13yrs

The Mulberry House School

An established independent school for
2-8 year olds, offering a stimulating and
caring environment that meets the needs
of individuals, while preparing them for
the next stage of their schooling at 4+
or 7+. Extended day, full and part time
places available.

For brochures and details of
open evenings please telephone

020 8452 7340

E-mail: tmhs@rmplc.co.uk.

7 Minster Road,
West Hampstead, NW2 3SD

Heathside Preparatory School
16 New End. 020 7794 5857
Co-ed $2^{1}/_{2}$-$13^{1}/_{2}$yrs

Hereward House School
14 Strathray Gardens. 020 7794 4820
Boys 4-13

Phoenix School
36 College Crescent. 020 7722 4433
Co-ed 3-7yrs

**Royal School Hampstead
(Royal Soldiers Daughters School)**
65 Rosslyn Hill. 020 7794 7708
Girls 4-18yrs (boarders from 7yrs)

St.Christopher's School
32 Belsize Lane. 020 7435 1521
Girls 4-11yrs

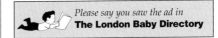

Please say you saw the ad in
The London Baby Directory

schools, preparatory and pre-prep (cont.)

St Mary's School, Hampstead
47 Fitzjohn's Avenue. 020 7435 1868
Boys 3-7yrs, Girls 3-11yrs

Sarum Hall
15 Eton Avenue. 020 7794 2261
Girls 3-11yrs

Southbank International School
16 Netherhall Gardens. 020 7431 1200
Co-ed 3-18yrs

South Hampstead High School
5 Netherhall Gardens. 020 7794 7198
Girls 4-11yrs
Senior school: 3 Maresfield Gardens.
020 7435 2899
11-18yrs

Trevor-Roberts Prep School
55-57 Eton Avenue. 020 7586 1444
Co-ed 5-13yrs

Village School
2 Parkhill Road. 020 7485 4673
4-11yrs

NW4
Hendon Preparatory School
20 Tenterden Grove. 020 8203 7727
Co-ed 2-13yrs

NW6
Broadhurst School
19 Greencroft Gardens. 020 7328 4280
Co-ed 2¹/₂-7yrs

Islamia Primary School
Salusbury Road. 020 7372 2532
5-16yrs

Rainbow Montessori School
13 Woodchurch Road. 020 7328 8986
5-11yrs

NW7
Goodwyn School
Hammers Lane, Mill Hill. 020 8959 3756
3-11yrs

Mill Hill Pre-Prep School
Winterstoke House, Wills Grove.
020 8959 6884
3-7yrs

Mount School
Milespit Hill, Mill Hill. 020 8959 3403
Girls 4-18yrs

NW8
Abercorn Place School
28 Abercorn Place. 020 7286 4785
Co-ed 2¹/₂-13yrs

American School in London
2-8 Loudoun Road. 020 7449 1200
Co-ed 4-18yrs

St Christina's RC Preparatory School
25 St Edmund's Terrace. 020 7722 8784
Boys 3-7yrs, Girls 3-11yrs+

St John's Wood Junior Prep School
St John's Hall, Lord's Roundabout.
020 7722 7149
Co-ed 3-8yrs

NW9

St Nicholas School
22 Salmon Street. 020 8205 7153
www.happychild.co.uk. Co-ed 2-11yrs

NW11
Goldershill School
666 Finchley Road. 020 8455 2589
Co-ed 2-7yrs

King Alfred School
Manor Wood, North End Road.
020 8457 5200
Co-ed 4-18yrs

SE3
Blackheath High School
Vanbrugh Park. 020 8853 2929
Girls 4-18yrs

Pointers Nursery + Prep
19 Stratheden Road, Blackheath.
020 8293 1331
Co-ed 2³/₄-11yrs. Full day

SE9
St Olave's Prep School
106-110 Southwood Road, New Eltham.
020 8829 8930
Co-ed 3-11yrs

SE12
Colfe's Prep School
Horn Park Lane. 020 8852 2283
Co-ed 3-11yrs

Riverston School
63-69 Eltham Road, Lee. 020 8318 4327
Co-ed 1-16yrs

SE19
Virgo Fidelis Prep School
Central Hill, Upper Norwood.
020 8653 2169. Co-ed 2-11yrs

SE21
Dulwich College Prep School
42 Alleyn Park. 020 8670 3217
Boys 3-13yrs, Girls 3-5yrs. Nursery in
Gallery Road

Oakfield Prep School
125-128 Thurlow Park Road. 020 8670 4206
Co-ed 2-11yrs

Rosemead Preparatory School
70 Thurlow Park Road. 020 8670 5865
Co-ed 3-11yrs

SE22
Alleyn's School
Townley Road, Dulwich. 020 8693 3457
Co-ed 4-18yrs

James Allen's Prep School
East Dulwich Grove. 020 8693 0374
Girls 4-11yrs, Boys 4-7yrs

SE24
Herne Hill School
127 Herne Hill. 020 7274 6336
3-7yrs

SE26
Sydenham High School
15 & 19 Westwood Hill. 020 8778 8737
Girls 4-18yrs

SW1
Eaton House School
3-5 Eaton Gate. 020 7730 9343
Boys 4-9yrs.

Eaton Square Prep School
79 Eccleston Square. 020 7931 9469
Co-ed 2½-11yrs

Eaton Square Pre-Prep School
30 Eccleston Street. 020 7823 6217
Co-ed 2½-6yrs

Francis Holland School
39 Graham Terrace. 020 7730 2971
Girls 4-18yrs

Garden House School
53 Sloane Gardens. 020 7730 1652
Co-ed 3-11yrs

Hill House School
17 Hans Place. 020 7584 1331
Co-ed 4-13yrs

SW3
Cameron House
4 The Vale. 020 7352 4040
Co-ed 4-11yrs

SW4
Eaton House, The Manor
58 Clapham Common Northside.
020 7924 6000
Co-ed 2½-5yrs; Boys-8yrs

Parkgate House School
80 Clapham Common Northside.
020 7350 2452
Co-ed 2½-11yrs

SW6
Fulham Prep
47a Fulham High Street. 020 7371 9911
Co-ed 5-13yrs

Kensington Preparatory School for Girls
596 Fulham Road. 020 7731 9300
Girls 4-11yrs

Sinclair House School
159 Munster Road. 020 7736 9182
Co-ed 2-8yrs

SW7
Falkner House Girls School
19 Brechin Place. 020 7373 4501
Co-ed 3-4yrs, Girls 4-11yrs

Glendower Preparatory School
87 Queen's Gate. 020 7370 1927
Girls 4-12yrs

Hampshire Schools
5 Wetherby Place. 020 7370 7081
Co-ed 3-6yrs

Hampshire Schools
63 Ennismore Gardens. 020 7584 3297
Co-ed 3-13yrs

Lycée Français Charles de Gaulle
35 Cromwell Road. 020 7584 6322
Co-ed 4-18yrs

schools, preparatory and pre-prep (cont.)

Queen's Gate School
133 Queen's Gate. 020 7589 3587
Girls 4-18yrs

Ravenstone House South Kensington
20-22 Queensberry Place. 020 7262 1190
2¹/₂-8yrs
See advert under nursery schools

St James Independent School
91 Queen's Gate. 020 7373 5638
Co-ed 4-10yrs

St Nicholas Preparatory School
23 Princes Gate. 020 7225 1277
Co-ed 3-13yrs

St Philip's School
6 Wetherby Place. 020 7373 3944
Boys 7-13yrs

Vale School
2 Elvaston Place. 020 7584 9515
Co-ed 4-11yrs

SW8
Newton Prep
149 Battersea Park Road. 020 7720 4091
3-13yrs

SW10
Parayhouse School
St John's, World's End, King's Road.
020 7352 2882
Co-ed 5-17yrs with learning difficulties

Redcliffe School
47 Redcliffe Gardens. 020 7352 9247
Girls 3-11yrs, Boys 3-8yrs

SW11
Dolphin School
106 Northcote Road. 020 7924 3472
Co-ed 4-11yrs

South London Montessori School
Trott Street, Battersea. 020 7738 9546
2¹/₂-12yrs

Thomas's Prep School
28-40 Battersea High Street. 020 7978 0900
Co-ed 4-13yrs

Thomas's Prep School
Battersea Church Road. 020 7978 0900

Thomas's Prep School
Broomwood Road. 020 7326 9300
Co-ed 4-13yrs

SW12
Broomwood Hall School
74 Nightingale Lane. 020 8673 1616
Boys 4-8yrs, Girls 4-13yrs

Hornsby House School
Hearnville Road. 020 8675 1255
Co-ed 3-11yrs

Woodentops Pre-Preparatory School & Kindergarten
The White House, 24 Thornton Road.
020 8674 9514
2¹/₂-11yrs

SW13
Colet Court
Lonsdale Road. 020 8748 3461
7-13yrs. Junior St Paul's

Harrodian
Lonsdale Road. 020 8748 6117
Co-ed 5-15yrs

SW14
Tower House School
188 Sheen Lane. 020 8876 3323
Boys 4-13yrs

SW15
Hall School Wimbledon
Stroud Crescent, Putney Vale. 020 8788 2370
Co-ed 3-11yrs
Senior school at 17 The Downs, SW20.
020 8879 9200. 11-16yrs

Hurlingham School
95 Deodar Road. 020 8874 7186
Co-ed 4-11yrs

Ibstock Place School
Clarence Lane, Roehampton. 020 8876 9991
Co-ed 3-16yrs

Lion House School
The Old Methodist Hall, Gwendolen
Avenue. 020 8780 9446
Co-ed 3-8yrs

Prospect House School
75 Putney Hill. 020 8780 0456
Co-ed 3-11yrs

S

Putney High School
35 Putney Hill. 020 8788 4886
Girls 4-18yrs

Putney Park School
11 Woodborough Road. 020 8788 8316
Boys 4-11yrs, Girls 4-16yrs

SW16
Streatham Hill & Clapham High School
Abbotswood Road. 020 8677 8400
Girls 3-10yrs. 11-18yrs senior school of nursery in Wavertree Road

SW17
Bertrum House School
290 Balham High Street. 020 8767 4051
2-8yrs

Finton House School
169-171 Trinity Road. 020 8682 0921
Co-ed 4-11yrs

SW18
Highfield School
256 Trinity Road. 020 8874 2778
Co-ed 2-11yrs

SW19
Kings College School
Southside, Wimbledon Common.
020 8255 5300
Boys 7-13yrs

Study Preparatory School
Wilberforce House, Camp Road,
Wimbledon Common. 020 8947 6969
Girls 4-11yrs

Willington School
Worcester Road, Wimbledon. 020 8944 7020
Boys 4-13yrs

Wimbledon High School
Mansel Road. 020 8971 0900
Girls 4-18yrs

Wimbledon House School
1b-1c Dorset Road. 020 8544 1523
Co-ed 3-11yrs

SW20
Rowans
19 Drax Avenue. 020 8946 8220
3-9yrs

Full listings for TW schools can be found in the Local Baby Directory: Surrey & S. Middlesex

TW9
Kew College
24-26 Cumberland Road, Kew, Richmond.
020 8940 2039
3-11yrs

Unicorn School
238 Kew Road, Richmond. 020 8948 3926
Co-ed 3-11yrs

TW10
King's House School
68 Kings Road, Richmond. 020 8940 1878
Boys 4-13yrs

TW12
Twickenham Preparatory School
43 High Street, Hampton. 020 8979 6216
Boys 4-13yrs, Girls 4-11yrs

W2
Connaught House School
47 Connaught Square, Hyde Park.
020 7262 8830
Boys 4-8yrs, Girls 4-11yrs

Hampshire Schools
9 Queensborough Terrace. 020 7229 7065
Co-ed 4-13yrs

Pembridge Hall School for Girls
18 Pembridge Square. 020 7229 0121
Girls 4-11yrs

Wetherby School
11 Pembridge Square. 020 7727 9581
Boys 4-8yrs

schools, preparatory and pre-prep (cont.)

W3
King Fahad Academy
Bromyard Avenue. 020 8743 0131
Muslim. Parallel classes for Boys and Girls
4-18yrs

International School of London
139 Gunnersbury Avenue. 020 8992 5823
Co-ed 4-18yrs. English + Arabic, etc.

W4
Chiswick and Bedford Park Prep School
Priory House, Priory Avenue. 020 8994 1804
Boys 4-8yrs, Girls 4-11yrs

Falcons Pre-Prep School
2 Burnaby Gardens. 020 8747 8393
Boys 3-8yrs

Orchard House School
16 Newton Grove. 020 8742 8544
Co-ed 3-11yrs

W5
Aston House School
1 Aston Road. 020 8566 7300
www.happychild.co.uk. Co-ed 2-11yrs

Clifton Lodge Prep School
8 Mattock Lane. 020 8579 3662
Boys 4-13yrs

Durston House School
12 Castlebar Road. 020 8997 0511
Boys 4-13yrs

Falcons School for Girls
15 Gunnersbury Avenue. 020 8992 5189
3-11yrs

Harvington School
20 Castlebar Road. 020 8997 1583
Girls 3-16yrs, Boys 3-5yrs

St Angelo Prep School
10 Montpelier Road. 020 8997 3209
4-11yrs

St Augustine's Priory
Hillcrest Road. 020 8997 2022
Girls 4-18yrs

St Benedict's Junior School
5 Montpelier Avenue. 020 8862 2050
Boys 4-11yrs

W6
Bute House School
Luxembourg Gardens. 020 7603 7381
Girls 4-11yrs

Larmenier Infant School
Great Church Lane. 020 8748 9444
3-7yrs

Ravenscourt Park Prep School
16 Ravenscourt Avenue. 020 8846 9153
Co-ed 4-11yrs

W7
Manor House School
16 Golden Manor, Hanwell. 020 8567 4101

W8
Hawkesdown House School
27 Edge Street. 020 7727 9090
Boys 3-8yrs

Lady Eden's School
39-41 Victoria Road. 020 7937 0583
Girls 3-11yrs

Thomas's Prep School
17-19 Cottesmore Gardens. 020 7361 6500
Co-ed 4-13yrs

W10
Bassett House School
60 Bassett Road. 020 8969 0313
Co-ed 3-8yrs

W11
Norland Place School
162-166 Holland Park Avenue.
020 7603 9103
Girls 4-11yrs, Boys 4-8yrs

Southbank International School
36-38 Kensington Park Road. 020 7229 8230
Co-ed 4-18yrs

W12
Bluesky Academy of Education & Arts
2a The Curve, Shepherds Bush.
020 8735 0552
$2^1/_2$-11yrs

W13
Avenue House School
70 The Avenue. 020 8998 9981
$2^1/_2$-11yrs. Full day

Notting Hill and Ealing High School
2 Cleveland Road. 020 8991 2165
Junior School: 020 8799 8484
Girls 5-18yrs

HAWKESDOWN HOUSE SCHOOL

A new independent school for boys aged 3 to 8, in Kensington, W8

opening in September 2001.

For further information:
Hawkesdown House School,
27 Edge Street, Kensington,
London, W8 7PN.
Telephone: 020 7727 9090.
Facsimile: 020 7727 9988.

sex choice

Materna S.A.
PO Box 21947, London SW3 2ZU.
020 7225 3234

sheep

Remember to avoid them if you're pregnant.

shoes

Sarah Page Sculpture
020 7207 0884
Your child's first shoe plated in copper or silver
See advert on page 17

N10
Foot in the Door
79-85 Fortis Green Road, Muswell Hill.
020 8444 9309

N16
Encore
53 Stoke Newington Church Street

NW3
Look Who's Walking
78 Heath Street. 020 7433 3855
Also clothing

NW8
Instep
45 St John's Wood High Street.
020 7722 7634

NW11
Brians Children's Shoes
2 Hallswelle Parade, Finchley Road.
020 8455 7001

SE3
Pares Footwear
24 Tranquil Vale, Blackheath. 020 8297 0785

SE19
Merlin Shoes
44 Westow Street. 020 8771 5194

SW6
French Sole
184 Munster Road. 020 7736 4780

Gillingham & Co
365 Fulham Palace Road. 020 7736 5757

Pollyanna
811 Fulham Road. 020 7731 0673

S

Visit us at
www.babydirectory.com

shoe shops (cont.)

SW7
Footsies
27 Bute Street. 020 7589 4787

SW13
Instep
80 Church Road. 020 8741 4114

SW15
Pied Piper
234 Upper Richmond Road. 020 8788 1635

SW19
Start-rite
47 High Street, Wimbledon. 020 8946 9735

TW9
The Shoe Station
3 Station Approach, Kew Gardens.
020 8940 9905

W1
Buckle My Shoe
19 St Christopher's Place. 020 7935 5589

W2
Pieton
9 Westbourne Grove. 020 7792 0707

W4
Chiswick Shoes
1 Devonshire Road. 020 8987 0525

W5
Stepping Out
106 Pitshanger Lane. 020 8810 6141

W11
Shoe Time
202 Kensington Park Road.
020 7727 7651

shopping crèches

Shop in peace!

in shopping centres:

NW3
Stay 'N' Play Crèche
02 Centre, 255 Finchley Road.
020 7435 9943

NW4
Nipperboat
Brent Cross Shopping Centre,
outside Mall 1, next to John Lewis.
020 8202 3667
2-8yrs

SW19
Centre Court Shopping Centre
Kids Club
4 Queens Road.
020 8944 8323 ext 23

in supermarkets:

E15
Safeway
The Grove, Stratford. 020 8555 0678

NW1
Safeway
Camden Goods Yard, Chalk Farm Road.
020 7267 9151

NW9
Safeway
Honey Pot Lane, Queensbury.
020 8204 1242

SE14
Stay 'N' Play Crèche
J. Sainsbury's Superstore,
263 New Cross Road, Lewisham.
020 7732 7444

single parents

(see also helplines)

Kids No Object
01243 543685

ski companies specialising in children

www.ifyouski.com
Best website with up-to-the-minute snow reports, virtual chalet tours, and special family offers
See advert under travel companies

Family Ski Company
01993 851084

Mark Warner
08708 480 482

Meriski
01451 843100

Simply Ski
020 8541 2207

Ski Beat
01243 780405 **Ski Company**
01451 843123

Ski Esprit
01252 618300

Ski Famille
01223 363777

Ski Olympic
01709 579999

Ski Scott Dunn
020 8767 0202

Ski Solutions
020 7471 7733
Ski holiday information and booking for all companies

Snowbizz Vacances
01778 341455

ski equipment rental and ski wear

Ski 3-Up
020 8669 1771

N12
Ski Occasions
020 8368 1212

NW3
Ski Wear Service
020 7435 0124
Buy or sell

SW6
47 Degrees
909 Fulham Road. 020 7731 5415
www.47degrees.com.

SW14
Ski Market
020 8741 7037
Second hand and new, 2 yrs+

SW15
47 Degrees Warehouse
164 Hurlingham Road. 020 7384 1979

W3
Ski Togs
020 8993 9883
Ring for opening times

ski slopes: artificial

Beckton Alpine Centre
Alpine Way, E6. 020 7511 0351

Hemel Ski Centre
St Albans Hill, Hemel Hempstead.
01442 241321
www.hemel-ski.co.uk. From 3yrs

Hillingdon Ski & Snowboard Centre
Park Road, Uxbridge. 01895 255183
From 3yrs

Wycombe Summit Ski & Snowboard
Abbey Barn Lane, High Wycombe.
01494 474711
3yrs+ (or size 9 shoe, 90cm ski)

S

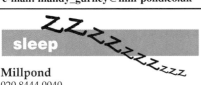

sleep

Millpond
020 8444 0040

The Good Sleep Guide
for you and your Baby
PO Box 5868, Forres IV36 1WH.
07020 922750

sleeping bags

Bonne Nuit
020 8871 1472
www.bonne-nuit.co.uk

Huggababy Natural Baby Products
Great House Barn, New Street, Talgarth,
Brecon, Powys. 01874 711629
www.huggababy.co.uk
See advert on page 78

Kuddlekit Ltd
99 Manor Road, Woodstock, Oxon.
01993 813854
www.kuddlekit.com

Sleepy Bunnies
01865 300310
www.sleepybunnies.com
See advert on page 78

Snuggle Sac
8 Bell Court, , Hurley, Berkshire SL6 5NA.
01628 824416

slimming clubs

Numbers are central information lines.
Call for details of your local class.

Rosemary Conley
Diet and Fitness Clubs
01509 620222

Slimming World
01773 521111

Weight Watchers
0345 123000

spanish

SW4
Anglo Spanish Nursery
152 Clapham Manor Street. 020 7622 5599
18mths-5yrs. Full day

SW6/W14
Isla Hispana
020 7488 0524

SW7
en español
48 Emperors Gate. 020 7603 9188
isfus@aol.com

Kensington International School
20 Queenberry Place. 020 7581 9357
Co-ed 18mths-10yrs

W6
Peques Nursery
138 Greyhound Road. 020 7385 0055
www.pequesspanishnursery.co.uk.
2-5yrs

W10
Spanish Day Nursery
317 Portobello Road. 020 8960 6661
2-5yrs. Full day

special needs

Special People
Palace for All, Schofield Road, N19.
020 7686 0253
special.people@virgin.net
Specialising in special needs

speech therapists

Karen Rivlin
Notting Hill Centre, 59/61 Ladbroke Grove,
W11. 020 7727 9551

Portland Hospital
205-209 Great Portland Street, W1.
020 7580 4400
www.theportlandhospital.com

sports facilities

(see also leisure centres, swimming pools)

Hammersmith and Fulham Council
Pools, fitness, music
See advert above

Sportsline
020 7222 8000
Information line

BABY SWIMMING

Swimming the natural way, without the use of bouyancy aids, for 0 - 4 years old. Surrey, Kent & London. Warm pools, small classes, in-pool instructor. Term start in Jan, April & Sept.

Aqua Tots
~naturally~
www.aquatots.com

020 8688 6488

swimming classes

(see also swimming pools)

Local swimming pools often run classes for aqua-natal, babies and young children.

Aquatots
020 8806 1515

Dolphin Club
020 8640 7232

Little Dippers
01273 328275

Little Dolphins
020 7751 1058

N20
Oakleigh Park School of Swimming
Oakleigh Road North. 020 8445 1911

South East
Superkids Swimming School
020 8693 3651

SE13
Lewisham Swim School
261 Lewisham High Street. 020 8690 2123

SE19
Amateur Swimming Association courses
Crystal Palace National Sports Centre.
020 8778 0131 ext 276
Ante/post aquanatal parent/baby, pre-school & after school swimming classes.

South West
South West Swimming School
020 8764 6161

SW18
Dolphin Swim Schools
020 8542 0931

SW1
Swimming Nature
Queen Mother Sports Centre,
23 Vauxhall Bridge Road. 020 7630 6871
www.swimmingnature.co.uk

SW4/SW12
Mighty Ducks Swimming School
020 8240 8657

W11
Swimming Nature
Kensington Sports Centre. 020 7221 6520
www.swimmingnature.co.uk

WC1
Dolphin Swimming Club
ULU Pool, Malet Street. 020 8349 1844
3yrs+

swimming pools

(see also health clubs with crèches, leisure centres)

E10
Leyton Leisure Lagoon
763 High Road, Leyton. 020 8558 8858

EC1
Finsbury Leisure Centre
Norman Street, Islington. 020 7253 2346

N1
Britannia Sports Centre
40 Hyde Road, Shoreditch. 020 7729 4485
Beach-style pool, wave machine, water slide

Cally Pool
229 Caledonian Road. 020 7278 1890
Dolphin slides, inflatable sessions.

N4
Rowans Leisure
10 Stroud Green Road, Finsbury Park.
020 8800 1950

N5
Highbury Pool
Highbury Crescent. 020 7704 2312
Children's float sessions, parties

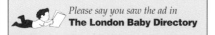

N8
Park Road Pools
Park Road. 020 8341 3567
Swimming classes, shallow pool, antenatal,
postnatal

N9
Lee Valley Leisure Centre
Picketts Lock Lane. 020 8345 6666

N15
Tottenham Green Leisure Centre
1 Philip Lane, Tottenham. 020 8489 5315
Fountains, beach, wave machine, play
tower

N19
Archway Leisure Centre
14 Macdonald Road, Archway.
020 7281 4105
Wave machine, slide, spa pool, river run

NW3
Swiss Cottage Sports Centre
Winchester Road. 020 7413 6501
Parent & toddler sessions

NW4
Barnet Copthall Pools
Great North Way, Hendon. 020 8457 9900
www.barnet-lifestyle.org.uk. Beach pool,
wildwater ride

NW10
Willesden Sports Centre
Donnington Road. 020 8459 6605
Crèche, many other sports facilities. Water
can be cold

SE1
Elephant & Castle Recreation Centre
22 Elephant & Castle. 020 7582 5505
Slides, splash pool, wave machine

SE5
Camberwell Leisure Centre
Artichoke Place, Camberwell Church Street.
020 7703 3024

SE8
Wavelengths Leisure Pool
Giffin Street, Deptford. 020 8694 1134
Wave machine, flumes, wildwater
channels, whirlpool, water cannons

SE9
Eltham Pools
Eltham Hill. 020 8859 0898

SE13
Ladywell Leisure Centre
261 Lewisham High Street. 020 8690 2123

SE18
Waterfront Leisure Centre
High Street, Woolwich. 020 8317 5000
Safari Oasis, anaconda slide, volcano, etc

SE22
Dulwich Leisure Centre
45 East Dulwich Road. 020 8693 1833

SE23
Forest Hill Leisure Centre
Dartmouth Road, Forest Hill. 020 8699 3096

SE26
The Bridge Leisure Centre
Kangley Bridge Road, Lower Sydenham.
020 8778 7158

SW1
Queen Mother Sports Centre
223 Vauxhall Bridge Road. 020 7630 5522
Classes for Mummy and Ducklings

SW3
Chelsea Sports Centre
Chelsea Manor Street. 020 7352 6985

SW9
Brixton Recreation Centre
Brixton Station Road. 020 7926 9779

SW11
Latchmere Leisure Centre
Burns Road, Battersea. 020 7207 8004

SW15
Putney Leisure Centre
Upper Richmond Road. 020 785 0388

SW16
Streatham Pool
384 Streatham High Road. 020 7926 6744

SW19
Wimbledon Leisure Centre
Latimer Road. 020 8542 1330
www.merton-leisure.co.uk

swimming pools (cont.)

TW8
Fountain Leisure Centre
658 Chiswick High Road. 020 8994 9596

TW9
Pools on the Park
Old Deer Park, Twickenham Road,
Richmond. 020 8940 0561

W1
Seymour Leisure Centre
Seymour Place. 020 7723 8091
Lessons

W2
Porchester Centre
Queensway. 020 7792 2919
Parent & toddler sessions, classes

W3
Acton Baths
Salisbury Street. 020 8992 8877

W4
New Chiswick Pool
Edensor Road. 020 8747 8811
Clean, simple pool. Good lessons

W10
Jubilee Sports Centre
Caird Street. 020 8960 9629
Babies classes, crèche

W11
Kensington Sports Centre
Walmer Road. 020 7727 9747
Learner pool, ducklings, crèche

W12
Janet Adegoke Leisure Centre
Bloemfontein Road. 020 8743 3401
Beach-style pool, wave machine, slides,
giant frog

W13
Gurnell Leisure Centre
Ruislip Road East. 020 8998 3241

■ *Berkshire*
Coral Reef
Nine Mile Ride, Bracknell. 01344 862525

swimming pools: outdoor

Usually only open during the summer
months.

N8
Park Road Outdoor Pools
See under swimming pools

N12
Finchley Lido
Great North Leisure Park, High Road,
North Finchley. 020 8343 9830
Indoor, very small outdoor pool

NW5
Parliament Hill Lido
Parliament Hill Fields, Gordon House
Road. 020 7485 3873

SE18
Charlton Lido
Hornfair Park, Woolwich. 020 8856 7180
July-Sept

SE24
Brockwell Park Lido
Brockwell Park, Dulwich Road.
020 7274 3088

SW16
Tooting Bec Lido
Tooting Bec Common, Tooting Bec Road.
020 8871 7198

TW9
Richmond Pools on the Park
See under swimming pools

TW12
Hampton Heated Open Air Pool
High Street, Hampton Court. 020 8979 9933

W2
Serpentine Lido
Hyde Park. 020 7298 2100

WC2
Oasis Sports Centre Outdoor Pool
32 Endell Street, Holborn. 020 7831 1804

Ideas and things to do!

tennis

Also check out your local leisure centre.

N1
Islington Tennis Centre
Market Road. 020 7700 1370. 4yrs+

N8
Holly Park Junior Tennis Club
Crouch End Playing Fields, Park Road.
020 8347 7550

NW3
Hampstead Heath Tennis
020 8348 9930

SW13
Rocks Lane Tennis Centre
Rocks Lane. 020 8876 8330

W4/W14
Will To Win Tennis Centre
020 8994 1466. 5yrs+

TENS machines

Pain relief without drugs.
Babycare TENS
108 George Lane, E18. 020 8532 9595

ObTens
2 Rosling Road, Horfield, Bristol.
0117 951 4110

TensCare
020 8547 1999

Trust Tens
265 Park Road, Kingston, Surrey.
020 8546 1616

theatres

(see also arts centres, drama)

Many theatres stage shows for children,
especially around Christmas.

Artsline
London's information and advice service
for disabled people on arts &
entertainment. 020 7388 2227
Also produce a booklet caled *'Play'* on
activities for disabled children (£2).

London Bubble
5 Elephant Lane. 020 7237 4434
Mobile arts company

Puppet Theatre Barge
020 7249 6876
Varying locations throughout the year

N1
Little Angel Theatre
14 Dagmar Passage, off Cross Street.
020 7226 1787

N6
Lauderdale House
Highgate Hill, Waterlow Park.
020 8348 8716

N7
Unicorn Theatre
St Mark's Studios, Chillingworth Road.
020 7700 0702

NW6
Tricycle Theatre
269 Kilburn High Road. 020 7328 1000

SE6
Lewisham Theatre
Catford. 020 8690 0002

SE8
Deptford Albany Theatre
Douglas Way, Deptford. 020 8692 4446

SW11
Battersea Arts Centre
Old Town Hall, Lavender Hill.
020 7223 2223
www.bac.org.uk

t

theatres (cont.)

SW17
Nomad Puppet Studio
37 Upper Tooting Road. 020 8767 4005

SW19
Polka Theatre for Children
240 The Broadway. 020 8543 4888
boxoffice@polkatheatre.com
www.polkatheatre.com

SW19
Colour House Theatre
Merton Abbey Mills, Watermill Way.
020 8542 6644
3yrs+

TW
Watermans Art Centre
40 High Street, Brentford. 020 8568 1176

W6
Lyric Theatre Hammersmith
King Street. 020 8741 2311

toy libraries

National Association of
Toy and Leisure Libraries
68 Churchway, NW1. 020 7387 9592
Send sae for list of closest toy library

N15
St Ann's Toy Library
Cissbury Road. 020 8800 4390

N17
Northumberland Park Women &
Children's Centre
Somerford Grove. 020 8808 9117

NW6
Talbot Toy Library
62 Chichester Road. 020 8537 8988
Also internet access

toy shops

(see also mail order: toys)

Early Learning Centre and Mothercare have
branches on many high streets.

www.toystoteach.com

N8
Soup Dragon
27 Topsfield Parade, Tottenham Lane,
Crouch End. 020 8348 0224

Word Play
1 Broadway Parade, Crouch End.
020 8347 6700

N10
Fagin's Toys
84 Fortis Green Road. 020 8444 0282

Never Never Land
3 Midhurst Parade, Fortis Green.
020 8883 3997

N16
route 73 kids
86 Stoke Newington Church Street.
020 7923 7873

NW1
Harvey Johns
16-20 Parkway. 020 7485 1718

NW2
Toys 'R' Us
Tilling Road. 020 8209 0019
Branches in Croydon, Enfield, Hayes Road

NW3
Happy Returns
36 Rosslyn Hill. 020 7435 2431

Kristin Baybars
7 Mansfield Road. 020 7267 0934

Toys, Toys, Toys
10-11 Northways Parade, Finchley Road.
020 7722 9821

NW8
J.J.Toys
138 St John's Wood High Street.
020 7722 4855

SE3
2nd Impressions Toys
10 Montpellier Vale, Blackheath.
020 8852 6192

SE21
Art, Stationers & Toyshop
31 Dulwich Village. 020 8693 5938

SE22
Soup Dragon
106 Lordship Lane. 020 8693 5575

SW1
Harrods
Knightsbridge. 020 7730 1234

SW3
Daisy & Tom
181 Kings Road. 020 7352 5000

Traditional Toys
53 Godfrey Street. 020 7352 1718

SW4
Cheeky Monkeys
24 Abbeville Road. 020 8673 5215
See advert on page 200

SW6
Cheeky Monkeys
94 New Kings Road. 020 7731 3031
See advert on page 200

Patrick's Toys & Games
107-111 Lillie Road. 020 7385 9864

SW7
tridias
25 Bute Street. 020 7584 2330

Toybox
12 Gloucester Road. 020 7591 6410

SW11
Q.T.Toys
90 Northcote Road. 020 7223 8637

SW13
Bug Zoo
Castelnau Road. 020 8741 4244

The Farmyard
63 Barnes High Street. 020 8332 0038

SW15
Domat Designs
3 Lacy Road, Putney. 020 8788 5715

SW15
Havanas Toy Box
Unit 3, Ground floor,
Putney Exchange Centre. 020 8780 3722

Tiny Set Toys
54 Lower Richmond Road. 020 8788 0392

SW17
Cheeky Monkeys
Bennet Court, 1 Bellevue Road.
020 8672 2025
See advert on page 200

TW
Little Wonders
3 York Street, Twickenham. 020 8255 6114

t

Unusual & traditional
childrens toys and gifts,
furniture, china,
dressing-up, hats etc.

94 New Kings Road
London SW6 4UL
020 7731 3031

202 Kensington Park Road
London W11 1NR
020 7792 9022

24 Abbeville Road
London SW4 9NH
020 8673 5215

1 Bellevue Road
London SW17 7EG
020 8672 2025

**Something for everyone
and
every occasion!**

toy shops (cont.)

W1
The Disney Store
140-144 Regent Street. 020 7287 6558
www.disney.com

Hamleys
188-196 Regent Street. 020 7494 2000
Also branches in Covent Garden and
Heathrow Airport

W2
The School Shop
31 Connaught Street. 020 7402 3406

W4
Snap Dragon
56 Turnham Green. 020 8995 6618

W5
Toy Stack
Ealing Broadway Centre. 020 8579 6526

The Disney Store
42C The Broadway Centre. 020 8567 6898

W6
Buttercups Children's Emporium
83 King Street. 020 8741 8184

W11
Cheeky Monkeys
202 Kensington Park Road. 020 7792 9022

W13
Beatties of London
72a Broadway. 020 8579 9959

Buttercups
75 Broadway

WC2
Peter Rabbit and Friends
Unit 42, The Market, Covent Garden.
020 7497 1777
www.charactergifts.com

toys

When I am grown to man's estate
I shall be very proud and great,
And tell the other girls and boys
Not to meddle with my toys.

R.L.Stevenson

travel companies specialising in children

(see also ski companies, travel with kids)

If You....
Ifyouski.com, ifyoudive.com,
ifyougolf.com...

Club Med
020 7581 1161
Brochures: 01455 852 202

Eurocamp
01606 787000

EuroVillages
01606 787776

First Choice
0870 750 0001

Mark Warner
08708 480 482

Sun Esprit
01252 618300

Sunsail
01705 222222

Thomson Holidays
0990 502555

VICTORIA PAGE
Est.1982

PRIVATE TUITION
Children 3yrs – 11+
Remedial Reading
Maths & English
Adult Students of English
Preparatory School &
Common Entrance

**07050
246 810
Fulham**

travel with kids

We don't (yet) have Baby Directories in the following cities, so try:

Amsterdam
Kids Gids

Edinburgh
Edinburgh for Under Fives

New York
City Baby

Paris
Le Paris des tout-petits

UK: *Local Baby Directories*
www.babydirectory.com
Guides to almost everywhere in the UK.
See order form at the front of the book or
ring our credit card hotline: 020 8742 8724

Family Travel Magazine
1 Hargrave Road, N19. 020 7272 7441

WWW.
BABY
directory.com
Order on line

tuition

Victoria Page Private Tuition
Fulham. 020 7381 9911
$2^{1}/_{2}$-11yrs
Scholarship, maths, English, reasoning,
remedial reading

Kumon Educational
0800 854 714
www.kumon.co.uk
See advert on page 92

Southgate Tutorial School
020 8446 5216
3-16yrs

The Tutoring Company
80 Perryn Road, W3. 020 8749 5279
3-18yrs

Vernice Gilbert
020 8994 2632

videos

Formative Years
Stonelands, Selsfield Road,
West Hoathly, West Sussex RH19 4QY.
01342 826555
www.formativeyears.co.uk
See advert under mail order: video

Getting Back
PO Box 1051, Oxford OX2 7YE.
01865 558833
www.gettingback.co.uk

Help I'm Having a Baby
01637 831001

water births

If planning a hospital delivery, check with your local hospital for their facilities and policies on water birth *(see hospitals: NHS and private)*. The following offer birth pool rentals.

Active Birth Centre
020 7482 5554

Splashdown
020 8422 9308

water exercise in pregnancy

Many local swimming pools run aqua-natal courses *(see swimming pools)*.

Chelsea Sports Centre
Chelsea Manor Street, Kings Road, SW3.
020 7352 6985

web sites

www.babydirectory.com
UK-wide Baby Directory, Encyclopaedia of Pregnancy & Birth, bookshop, nursery goods shop, free medical advice, and much much more…

Oh, are there some other sites?
OK… But with the current rate of dotcom burnout, some of these may not be around by the time you click on them. But we will!

www.b4baby.com

www.babybsmart.com

www.babydirectory.com

www.babyworld.co.uk

www.flametree.co.uk

www.ukparents.co.uk

www.urbia.com

Chosen Inheritance Ltd

Who would look after your young
ones if you weren't around?

PARENTS NEED WILLS !!

Friendly fixed price service
Call free for a quote
0800 917 4542

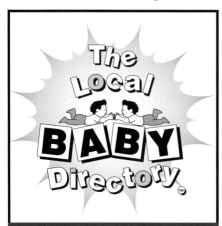

The
LOCAL

BABY
Directory™

Franchise
Opportunities

020 8742 8724

or e-mail us
editor@babydirectory.com

W

welsh

We now have a South Wales Baby
Directory! See the order form for details.

**Welsh Playgroup/Ysgol Gymraeg
Llundain**
c/o Stonebridge Primary School,
Shakespeare Avenue, NW10. 020 8965 3585
www.cymraeg@llundain.freeserve.co.uk

wills

Chosen Inheritance
Victoria House, 2 Victoria Terrace,
Ealing Green, W5. 020 8840 4080
www.choseninheritance.co.uk

working opportunities

Baby Directory
Looking to run a franchise? Experience in
telesales? Got a few hours a week? Call us
on 020 8742 8724 to discuss your career
development centred around your
children's needs.

Bravado Maternity Nursing Bras
020 8459 2910
See advert under breastfeeding accessories

Kumon Educational
0800 854 714
www.kumon.co.uk
See advert on page 92

Ragged Bears
01483 481790

Usborne Books at Home
01938 590021
www.usborne.com

Working Options
14-16 Hamilton Road, W5. 020 8932 1462
www.working-options.co.uk

yoga in pregnancy or for children

(see also antenatal teachers)

N7
Yoga Junction
97-99 Seven Sisters Road. 020 7263 3113
www.yogajunction.com

N16
Yogahome
Bliss Studios, 11 Allen Road.
020 7249 2425
Also baby massage, yoga for kids

N19
Active Birth Centre
25 Bickerton Road. 020 7482 5554
Send sae for information about a local
teacher

NW3
Triyoga
Erskine Road, Primrose Hill.
020 7483 3344
www.triyoga.com

Yvonne Moore Birth Preparation
020 7794 2056

SE24/SW19/SW20
Exercise for Pregnancy and Birth
020 8287 5411

SW12
The Art of Health + Yoga Centre
020 8682 1800. Also for babies

SW14
Studioflex
26-28 Priests Bridge. 020 8878 4073

SW19
Yogabugs
020 8944 7124. For kids

W1
Care in pregnancy
The Portland Hospital for Women and
Children, 205-209 Great Portland Street.
020 7390 8061

W8
The Grove Health Centre
182-184 Kensington Church Street.
020 7221 2266

The Life Centre
15 Edge Street. 020 7221 4602
See advert under complementary health

W10
Innergy Yoga Centre
Acorn Hall, East Row. 020 8968 1178

W11
Yoga for Pregnant and Postnatal
Lolly Stirk. 01323 422054

W13
Ella van Meelis
020 8537 9258
ellaVanMeelis@aol.com

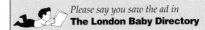
y

ZOOS

(see also farms, nature reserves, outings, parks)

■ *London*
Battersea Park Zoo
Battersea Park, North Carriage Drive, SW11.
Lots of monkeys, cow, smaller mammals, kangaroos etc. Poor café

London Zoo
Regents Park, NW1. 020 7722 3333

■ *Bedfordshire*
Whipsnade Wild Animal Park
Whipsnade, nr Dunstable. 0990 200123
www.whipsnade.co.uk

Woburn Safari Park
Woburn. 01525 290407
Drive-through wildlife park. M1 Jct 12 or 13

■ *East Sussex*
Drusilla's Park
Alfriston. 01323 870234
One mile N of Alfriston, on A27 between Eastbourne & Brighton

■ *Hampshire*
Marwell Zoological Park
Colden Common, Winchester. 01426 943163
B2177, 6 miles south of Winchester from Jct 11, M3.

■ *Hertfordshire*
Paradise Wildlife Park
White Stubbs Lane, Broxbourne.
01992 470490

Oxfordshire
Cotswold Wildlife Park
Burford. 01993 823006
On A361. 120 acres, rhinos, etc

■ *Surrey*
Birdworld and Underwater World
Holt Pound, Farnham. 01420 22140

notes

Z

index

notes

(CREDIT CARD)
hotline
020 8742 8724

1. New Baby Directory out every Spring—
remember get the new one

2. Must tell my friends to get
their own copies

3. Sam's having a baby must buy her a copy
but which edition — so many to choose from

4. Visit www.babydirectory.com
& see what all the fuss is about!!!!